Elixir on the Chain

A Developer's Guide for Building High-Performance Blockchain Network

Corbin Husman

Copyright © 2024 Corbin Husman

All rights reserved. No part of this book may be reproduced, stored in a retrieval system, or transmitted, in any form or by any means, electronic, mechanical, photocopying, recording, or otherwise, without the prior written permission of the author, except in the case of brief quotations embodied in critical reviews and certain other noncommercial uses permitted by copyright law.

Disclaimer

This book is for educational and informational purposes only. It is not intended as financial, legal, or investment advice. The author and publisher do not guarantee accuracy, completeness, or timeliness of the information and are not responsible for errors or omissions.

Cryptocurrency and blockchain investments are highly speculative and involve significant risk. The author and publisher are not liable for any losses or damages incurred.

The views expressed are those of the author and do not reflect the publisher's views. Specific product or company mentions do not constitute endorsements.

Readers should conduct their own research and consult qualified professionals before making financial or investment decisions related to blockchain technology or cryptocurrencies.

Table of Contents

Preface..7
Chapter 1: Introduction to Blockchain................................... 9
   1.1 What is Blockchain?... 9
   1.2 Key Characteristics of Blockchain.............................. 12
   1.3 Types of Blockchains... 15
   1.4 Blockchain Use Cases.. 19
   1.5 Why Elixir for Blockchain?.. 25
Chapter 2: Elixir Fundamentals..29
   2.1 Basic Syntax and Data Types..................................... 29
   2.2 Functional Programming Concepts............................ 32
   2.3 Processes and Concurrency......................................37
   2.4 OTP (Open Telecom Platform)................................... 41
   2.5 Error Handling and Fault Tolerance........................... 45
Chapter 3: Smart Contracts with Elixir................................ 49
   3.1 Understanding Smart Contracts................................. 49
   3.2 Smart Contract Languages.. 52
   3.3 Elixir and Smart Contracts... 57
   3.4 Security Considerations for Smart Contracts..............60
Chapter 4: Data Structures and Algorithms for Blockchain............. 63
   4.1 Hashing Algorithms..63
   4.2 Merkle Trees... 66
   4.3 Cryptographic Signatures and Digital Wallets............ 70
   4.4 Efficient Data Handling in Blockchain......................... 75
Chapter 5: Designing a Blockchain Network....................... 79
   5.1 Blockchain Architecture... 79
   5.2 Consensus Mechanisms in Elixir................................ 82
   5.3 Node Communication and Networking...................... 86
   5.4 Data Serialization and Storage.................................. 91
Chapter 6: Implementing a Basic Blockchain in Elixir....................95
   6.1 Project: Building a Simple Blockchain........................ 95
   6.2 Creating Blocks and Transactions.............................. 98
   6.3 Implementing a Basic Consensus Mechanism.......... 101

    6.4 Testing and Debugging.. 105
Chapter 7: Advanced Blockchain Features.. 109
    7.1 State Channels and Off-Chain Transactions.......................... 109
    7.2 Cross-Chain Interoperability.. 113
    7.3 Privacy-Enhancing Techniques.. 117
    7.4 Decentralized Storage (IPFS)... 121
Chapter 8: Building Decentralized Applications (DApps)............... 126
    8.1 Introduction to DApps.. 126
    8.2 Connecting Elixir Blockchain to Front-End Interfaces............. 130
    8.3 Example DApp Implementations... 135
Chapter 9: Deploying and Scaling Your Blockchain....................... 141
    9.1 Deployment Strategies... 141
    9.2 Cloud Platforms and Containerization...................................... 144
    9.3 Performance Optimization and Scaling.................................... 148
    9.4 Monitoring and Maintenance... 151
Chapter 10: The Future of Elixir and Blockchain............................ 157
    10.1 Emerging Trends in Blockchain.. 157
    10.2 Elixir's Role in the Blockchain Ecosystem............................. 162
Conclusion... 165

Preface

When I first started exploring blockchain, I was immediately drawn to its potential to revolutionize how we interact and do business online. But as I delved deeper, I realized that many blockchain projects faced challenges with performance, scalability, and maintainability. That's when I discovered the magic of Elixir. With its focus on concurrency, fault-tolerance, and functional programming, Elixir provides an ideal foundation for building robust and efficient blockchain systems. I wrote this book because I believe that Elixir and blockchain are a match made in code heaven, and I want to share that excitement with you.

This book aims to provide a comprehensive and practical guide to building blockchain networks and decentralized applications using Elixir. We'll start with the fundamentals of blockchain and Elixir, then move on to designing and implementing your own blockchain from scratch. We'll also explore advanced topics like smart contracts, state channels, and decentralized storage, and show you how to build real-world DApps. By the end of this book, you'll have the skills and confidence to create your own blockchain solutions and contribute to the exciting future of decentralized technology.

This book is written for developers who have some experience with Elixir and are interested in learning how to apply their skills to blockchain development. Whether you're a seasoned Elixir pro or just starting out, you'll find valuable insights and practical guidance within these pages.

No prior blockchain experience is required, but a basic understanding of programming concepts and data structures will be helpful.

The book is divided into three parts:

- Part I: Foundations: We'll lay the groundwork by covering the essentials of blockchain technology and Elixir programming.
- Part II: Building Blockchain Networks: This is where things get really interesting! You'll learn how to design and implement your own blockchain network using Elixir.
- Part III: Deployment and Beyond: We'll explore advanced topics and show you how to deploy and scale your blockchain applications.

Each chapter builds upon the previous one, guiding you through the process of becoming a proficient blockchain developer with Elixir. You'll find plenty of code examples, practical exercises, and real-world case studies to help you solidify your understanding.

So, grab your favorite beverage, fire up your code editor, and get ready to embark on an exciting adventure into the world of Elixir and blockchain! I'm thrilled to have you along for the ride, and I can't wait to see what amazing things you create. Let's get started!

Chapter 1: Introduction to Blockchain

We'll kick things off with the basics! Before we dive headfirst into building blockchain applications with Elixir, we need to make sure we're all on the same page about what blockchain actually *is*. Don't worry, I'm not going to bore you with dry technical jargon. We'll keep things light and conversational, just like two developers chatting over a cup of coffee (or tea, if that's your thing!).

1.1 What is Blockchain?

You've probably heard the term "Blockchain" thrown around a lot, maybe in relation to Bitcoin or other cryptocurrencies. But what *is* it, really? At its core, a blockchain is a special kind of database. Now, I know what you might be thinking: "A database? That sounds boring!" But trust me, this is no ordinary database. It has some unique properties that make it incredibly powerful and secure.

Think of a traditional database like a ledger kept by a single company or organization. This company has complete control over the data – they can add, delete, or modify records as they see fit. With a blockchain, however, things are different. Instead of being stored in one central location, the data is distributed across a network of computers.[2] It's like having a shared ledger where everyone has a copy, and everyone can see the transactions that take place.

But here's where it gets really interesting. Each transaction, or piece of data, is grouped together into a "block."[3] These blocks are then linked together in a chronological "chain," using cryptography to ensure that they cannot be tampered with.[4] Once a block is added to the chain, it's there forever – immutable and permanent.[5]

Let's illustrate this with a simple analogy:

Imagine a group of friends keeping track of their shared expenses in a notebook. Every time someone pays for something, they write it down in the notebook. At the end of the month, they add up all the expenses and figure out who owes what. This notebook is like a traditional database – it's centralized and can be easily modified.

Now, imagine instead that each friend has their own copy of the notebook. Every time someone makes a purchase, they record it in their own notebook and then share it with everyone else. Each entry is also marked with a special code (like a digital signature) to ensure its authenticity. Once everyone agrees that the entry is valid, it's added to a new "page" in the notebook, and everyone updates their copy. This shared, tamper-proof notebook is similar to a blockchain.

Key Concepts:

- Distributed Ledger: The database is not stored in a single location but is distributed across a network of computers.[6]

- Blocks: Transactions are grouped together into "blocks" of data.[7]
- Chain: Blocks are linked together chronologically, forming a chain.[8]
- Immutability: Once a block is added to the chain, it cannot be altered or deleted.
- Cryptography: Mathematical techniques are used to secure the data and ensure its integrity.[9]

Why is this important?

The decentralized and immutable nature of blockchain makes it incredibly secure and transparent.[10] Because the data is distributed across many computers, there's no single point of failure. If one computer goes down, the network can still function. And because the data is tamper-proof, you can be confident that it hasn't been altered or manipulated.

Real-World Example:

One of the most well-known examples of blockchain technology is Bitcoin.[11] Bitcoin uses a blockchain to record all transactions, ensuring that no one can spend the same Bitcoin twice.[12] This eliminates the need for a central authority like a bank to manage the currency.

While cryptocurrencies like Bitcoin and Ethereum are perhaps the most popular applications of blockchain, the technology has far broader potential. It can be used to track goods in a supply chain, verify digital identities, secure medical records, and even facilitate voting systems.[13]

1.2 Key Characteristics of Blockchain

Let's discuss the key characteristics that make it such a revolutionary technology. These are the features that set it apart from traditional databases and enable its unique capabilities.

1. Decentralization

This is a big one. In a traditional database system, all the data is stored in a central location, usually controlled by a single organization. This creates a single point of failure – if that central database is compromised, the entire system is at risk.

Blockchain, on the other hand, is decentralized. The data is not stored in one place but is distributed across a network of computers. Think of it like a network of peers, each holding a copy of the ledger. This means there's no single entity in control, and no single point of failure. If one computer in the network goes down, the others can still maintain the integrity of the blockchain.

This decentralized nature has several important implications:

- Fault Tolerance: The system is more resilient to failures and attacks.
- Censorship Resistance: No single entity can control or censor the data on the blockchain.
- Transparency: Everyone on the network has access to the same information.

2. Immutability

Once a block of data is added to the blockchain, it cannot be altered or deleted. This is a crucial feature that ensures the integrity and trustworthiness of the data.

How is this achieved? Through the magic of cryptography! Each block in the chain is linked to the previous block using a unique cryptographic hash. This hash acts like a digital fingerprint – any change to the data in the block would result in a completely different hash, breaking the chain.

This immutability has significant benefits:

- Data Integrity: You can be confident that the data on the blockchain has not been tampered with.
- Auditability: It's easy to track changes and verify the history of transactions.
- Trust: Participants can trust that the data is accurate and reliable.

3. Transparency

In most blockchain systems, the data is publicly accessible. Anyone can view the transactions that have taken place on the blockchain. This transparency promotes accountability and trust among participants.

Of course, there are also privacy-focused blockchains that use cryptographic techniques to protect sensitive information. But even in these systems, the underlying rules and mechanisms are transparent.

4. Security

Blockchain uses cryptography to secure the data and prevent unauthorized access. This includes:

- Hashing: Creating unique fingerprints for each block of data.
- Digital Signatures: Verifying the authenticity of transactions.
- Consensus Mechanisms: Ensuring that all participants agree on the state of the blockchain.

These security measures make it extremely difficult for malicious actors to tamper with the blockchain or steal data.

Real-World Example:

Consider a supply chain tracking system built on a blockchain. Each time a product changes hands, a record is added to the blockchain. This record might include information about the product's origin, manufacturing date, and current location. Because the blockchain is immutable and transparent, all participants in the supply chain can trust the authenticity of the data and track the product's journey with confidence.

Code Example (Conceptual):

While we haven't delved into specific code yet, here's a simplified conceptual example to illustrate how hashing works in a blockchain:

```python
# Imagine a function that calculates the hash of a block of data

def calculate_hash(data):
```

```
    # This is a simplified representation, actual
hash functions are more complex

    hash_value = some_hashing_algorithm(data)

    return hash_value

# Create a block of data

block1_data = {"transaction": "Alice sends 10
coins to Bob"}

# Calculate the hash of the block

block1_hash = calculate_hash(block1_data)

# Create a new block, linking it to the previous
block's hash

block2_data = {"transaction": "Bob sends 5 coins
to Carol", "previous_hash": block1_hash}

# Calculate the hash of the new block

block2_hash = calculate_hash(block2_data)

# ... and so on, creating a chain of blocks
```

In this example, you can see how each block is linked to the previous block's hash. Any change to the data in a block would result in a different hash, breaking the chain and alerting the network to a potential tampering attempt.

1.3 Types of Blockchains

Now that you're familiar with the core characteristics of blockchain, let's talk about the different flavors it comes in. You see, not all blockchains are created equal. They can vary significantly in terms of who can participate, how they operate, and what they're used for. Understanding these different types is crucial for choosing the right blockchain solution for your specific needs.

1. Public Blockchains

Think of a public blockchain like a bustling city square – open to everyone and anyone. You don't need permission to join, participate, or view the transactions happening within. Bitcoin and Ethereum are prime examples of public blockchains.

Here's a breakdown of their key features:

- **Permissionless:** No one controls who can join the network or participate in the consensus process (the way the network agrees on the validity of transactions).
- **Transparent:** All transactions are visible to everyone on the network, promoting accountability and openness.
- **Secure:** Secured by cryptography and a distributed network of nodes, making them extremely difficult to manipulate.
- **Incentivized:** Often use economic incentives (like mining rewards in Bitcoin) to encourage participation and secure the network.

Use Cases:

Public blockchains are well-suited for applications where transparency, security, and censorship resistance are paramount. This includes:

- Cryptocurrencies: Facilitating peer-to-peer transactions without intermediaries like banks.
- Decentralized Finance (DeFi): Building financial applications on a blockchain, such as lending platforms and decentralized exchanges.
- Non-Fungible Tokens (NFTs): Representing unique digital assets like artwork, collectibles, and in-game items.

2. Private Blockchains

Now, let's shift gears and consider a private blockchain. Imagine this as a private club with restricted access. Only authorized individuals or organizations can join the network and participate in its operations.

Key characteristics of private blockchains:

- Permissioned: Access is controlled by a central authority or a group of administrators.
- Controlled: Rules and governance are determined by the organization(s) managing the blockchain.
- Efficient: Transactions can be processed faster and with lower costs compared to public blockchains, as the network is smaller and more controlled.
- Privacy: Offers greater privacy as transactions are only visible to authorized participants.

Use Cases:

Private blockchains are often used within organizations or consortia to improve efficiency, security, and transparency. This includes:

- Supply Chain Management: Tracking goods and products within a company or across a group of partners.
- Healthcare: Securely managing patient data within a hospital network.
- Financial Institutions: Streamlining internal processes and reducing transaction costs.

3. Consortium Blockchains

Consortium blockchains can be thought of as a hybrid between public and private blockchains. They are typically governed by a group of organizations, each with its own set of permissions and responsibilities.

Key features:

- Semi-Decentralized: Control is shared among a group of organizations rather than a single entity.
- Permissioned: Access is restricted to members of the consortium.
- Scalable: Can handle a larger number of transactions compared to fully private blockchains.
- Collaborative: Facilitates collaboration and data sharing among different organizations.

Use Cases:

Consortium blockchains are often used in industries where collaboration and trust among different organizations are crucial. This includes:

- Industry Consortia: Sharing data and coordinating activities within a specific industry.

- Research and Development: Facilitating collaboration among research institutions.
- Government Services: Improving efficiency and transparency in government operations.

Selecting the appropriate blockchain type depends on your specific needs and goals. Consider factors like:

- Network Size: How many participants will be involved?
- Privacy: How important is data confidentiality?
- Performance: What level of transaction throughput is required?
- Governance: Who should have control over the network?

By carefully evaluating these factors, you can choose the blockchain type that best aligns with your requirements.

1.4 Blockchain Use Cases

You're probably starting to see that blockchain is more than just a buzzword. It's a powerful technology with the potential to transform a wide range of industries. Let's explore some real-world use cases where blockchain is already making a difference, and where it holds immense promise for the future.

1. Supply Chain Management

Ever wonder how products travel from the factory floor to your doorstep? It's a complex journey involving multiple parties, from manufacturers and suppliers to distributors and retailers. Traditional supply chains often lack transparency, making it difficult to track products, verify their authenticity, and ensure ethical sourcing.

This is where blockchain comes in. By recording every step of a product's journey on an immutable ledger, blockchain brings transparency and accountability to the supply chain.

Here's how it works:

- Each product is assigned a unique digital identity on the blockchain.
- Every time the product changes hands, a record is added to the blockchain, including information like location, timestamp, and responsible party.
- This creates an auditable trail that allows anyone to track the product's journey from origin to destination.

Benefits:

- Improved Traceability: Easily track products and identify potential bottlenecks or delays.
- Enhanced Transparency: Verify the authenticity and origin of products, combating counterfeiting and fraud.
- Increased Efficiency: Streamline processes and reduce paperwork by automating data recording and sharing.
- Ethical Sourcing: Ensure products are sourced from responsible and sustainable suppliers.

Example:

Walmart uses a blockchain-based system to track the origin and movement of mangoes throughout its supply chain.

This allows them to quickly identify the source of any contaminated products, preventing widespread outbreaks and ensuring food safety.

2. Healthcare

The healthcare industry faces numerous challenges, including data security, interoperability, and patient privacy. Blockchain[1] offers solutions to these issues by providing a secure and transparent platform for managing patient data.

Here's how it can be applied:

- Electronic Health Records (EHRs): Securely store and share patient data on a blockchain, giving patients greater control over their information and improving interoperability between healthcare providers.
- Clinical Trials: Enhance the integrity and transparency of clinical trials by recording data on a blockchain, preventing manipulation and ensuring accurate results.
- Drug Traceability: Track the movement of pharmaceuticals through the supply chain, combating counterfeit drugs and ensuring patient safety.

Benefits:

- Enhanced Security: Protect sensitive patient data from unauthorized access and breaches.
- Improved Interoperability: Facilitate seamless data sharing between healthcare providers.

- Increased Efficiency: Streamline administrative processes and reduce costs.
- Patient Empowerment: Give patients greater control over their health information.

Example:

The Medicalchain project uses blockchain to create a secure and decentralized platform for managing patient health records, allowing patients to grant access to their data to specific healthcare providers.

3. Finance

The financial industry is ripe for disruption by blockchain technology. Traditional financial systems often involve complex processes, high transaction fees, and intermediaries like banks. Blockchain offers the potential to streamline these processes, reduce costs, and increase efficiency.

Use Cases:

- Cross-Border Payments: Facilitate faster and cheaper international money transfers.
- Trade Finance: Simplify and automate trade finance processes, reducing paperwork and delays.
- Know Your Customer (KYC) and Anti-Money Laundering (AML): Create a secure and efficient system for verifying customer identities and preventing financial crime.

Benefits:

- Reduced Costs: Eliminate intermediaries and reduce transaction fees.
- Increased Speed: Settle transactions faster, improving efficiency.
- Enhanced Security: Improve security and reduce the risk of fraud.
- Greater Transparency: Provide a clear and auditable record of financial transactions.

Example:

Ripple uses blockchain technology to enable fast and low-cost cross-border payments for banks and financial institutions.

4. Voting and Governance

Blockchain can be used to create secure and transparent voting systems that are resistant to fraud and manipulation.

Here's how it works:

- Each voter is assigned a unique digital identity on the blockchain.
- Votes are recorded as transactions on the blockchain, ensuring they cannot be altered or deleted.
- The transparency of the blockchain allows for public auditing of the voting process.

Benefits:

- Increased Security: Prevent voter fraud and manipulation.

- Enhanced Transparency: Provide a clear and auditable record of votes.
- Improved Accessibility: Facilitate remote voting and increase voter participation.

Example:

Follow My Vote is a platform that uses blockchain technology to create secure and verifiable online voting systems.

5. Digital Identity

Blockchain can be used to create secure and verifiable digital identities, giving individuals greater control over their personal information and reducing the risk of identity theft.

Here's how it works:

- Individuals can store their identity information on a blockchain, creating a secure and tamper-proof digital identity.
- They can then selectively share their information with others, such as employers or service providers.

Benefits:

- Enhanced Security: Reduce the risk of identity theft and fraud.
- Increased Privacy: Give individuals greater control over their personal information.
- Improved Efficiency: Streamline identity verification processes.

Example:

Civic is a platform that uses blockchain technology to provide secure and verifiable digital identity solutions.

These are just a few examples of the many ways blockchain can be used to transform various industries. As the technology continues to evolve, we can expect to see even more innovative applications emerge.

1.5 Why Elixir for Blockchain?

You've seen the potential of blockchain, and now you're ready to start building. But with so many programming languages out there, why choose Elixir for your blockchain projects? Well, let me tell you, Elixir has some unique characteristics that make it a fantastic choice for tackling the challenges of blockchain development.

1. Concurrency

Blockchain networks are inherently distributed. They involve multiple nodes communicating and processing transactions concurrently. This requires a language that can handle concurrency efficiently, and Elixir excels in this area.

Elixir is built on the Erlang virtual machine (BEAM), which is renowned for its lightweight processes and ability to handle massive concurrency. Instead of relying on traditional threads, which can be resource-intensive, Elixir uses lightweight processes that communicate through message passing. This allows you to build highly concurrent systems that can handle a large number of transactions and interactions without breaking a sweat.

Imagine a busy coffee shop. In a traditional threaded system, each customer would be like a thread, requiring a significant amount of resources. In Elixir, each customer would be like a lightweight process, efficiently managed by the system. This means the coffee shop (your blockchain application) can serve many more customers (transactions) smoothly and efficiently.

2. Fault Tolerance

In a distributed system like a blockchain, things can go wrong. Network connections can drop, nodes can fail, and unexpected errors can occur. Elixir embraces a "let it crash" philosophy, meaning that instead of trying to prevent all errors, it provides mechanisms for isolating and recovering from them gracefully.

Elixir applications are built using OTP (Open Telecom Platform), a framework that provides tools for building robust and fault-tolerant systems. OTP processes are supervised, meaning that if one process crashes, a supervisor process can restart it, ensuring that the system as a whole remains stable.

This fault tolerance is crucial for blockchain applications, where downtime can be costly and even compromise the integrity of the network.

3. Functional Programming

Elixir is a functional programming language. This means that functions are treated as first-class citizens, and data is immutable. These characteristics have significant benefits for blockchain development:

- Immutability: In blockchain, data integrity is paramount. Elixir's immutability ensures that once data is created, it cannot be modified, preventing accidental or malicious alterations.
- Code Clarity: Functional programming promotes code that is easier to reason about, test, and maintain. This is crucial for building complex blockchain systems where bugs can have serious consequences.

4. Scalability

As blockchain networks grow, they need to handle an increasing number of transactions and users. Elixir's concurrency and fault-tolerance features make it highly scalable, allowing your blockchain applications to grow with the network.

Elixir's ability to handle massive concurrency means that your application can process a large number of transactions simultaneously. And its fault-tolerance ensures that the system can remain stable even under heavy load.

Real-World Example:

A company building a blockchain-based supply chain solution might choose Elixir because of its ability to handle the high volume of transactions generated by tracking goods across a complex network. Elixir's fault-tolerance would also be crucial to ensure that the system remains reliable and available, even if individual nodes experience issues.

Code Example (Conceptual):

While we'll get into more detailed code examples later, here's a simple illustration of how Elixir handles concurrency with processes:

```elixir
# Spawn a new process that prints "Hello from a process!"

spawn(fn -> IO.puts("Hello from a process!") end)

# Continue executing other code concurrently

IO.puts("Hello from the main process!")
```

In this example, spawn creates a new lightweight process that executes the code within the function. This process runs concurrently with the main process, allowing the application to perform multiple tasks simultaneously.

Elixir's combination of concurrency, fault-tolerance, functional programming, and scalability makes it a powerful tool for building robust, efficient, and reliable blockchain applications. As you progress through this book, you'll gain the skills and knowledge to harness these features and create your own blockchain solutions.

Chapter 2: Elixir Fundamentals

It's time to get our hands dirty with some Elixir! Don't worry, I won't overwhelm you with technical jargon. We'll explore the fundamentals in a friendly, conversational way, just like two programmers geeking out over a new language.

2.1 Basic Syntax and Data Types

Let's get you comfortable with the nuts and bolts of Elixir – its syntax and data types. Think of this as learning the alphabet and vocabulary of a new language. Once you grasp these fundamentals, you'll be well on your way to writing expressive and powerful Elixir code.

One of the things I love about Elixir is its clean and readable syntax. It borrows some ideas from Ruby, so if you've dabbled in Ruby before, you'll notice some similarities. But even if you're coming from a different programming background, don't worry – Elixir is designed to be approachable and easy to learn.

Variables

In Elixir, we use variables to store data. Think of them like labeled boxes where you can put different types of information. To assign a value to a variable, we use the = sign, like this:

```
Elixir

my_number = 10

my_name = "Alice"
```

Here, we've created two variables: `my_number` holds the integer value `10`, and `my_name` stores the string `"Alice"`. Simple, right?

Data Types

Elixir offers a variety of data types to represent different kinds of information. Let's explore some of the most common ones:

- Integers: These are whole numbers, like `10`, `-5`, `0`, and `1000`. You can use them to represent quantities, counts, or any other numerical data that doesn't require decimal points.
- Floats: When you need to work with numbers that have decimal points, you'll use floats. Examples include `3.14`, `-2.5`, and `0.001`.
- Booleans: These represent truth values – `true` or `false`. They're often used in conditional statements and logical operations.
- Atoms: Atoms are like named constants. They start with a colon `:` and are used to represent specific values or states. For example, `:ok` might indicate a successful operation, while `:error` could signal a problem.
- Strings: Strings are sequences of characters enclosed in double quotes. You'll use them to store text, like `"Hello, Elixir!"` or `"This is a string"`.

- Lists: Lists are ordered collections of elements. They can hold any type of data, and you can add, remove, or modify elements. For example, [1, 2, 3] is a list of integers, while ["apple", "banana", "cherry"] is a list of strings.
- Tuples: Tuples are similar to lists, but they have a fixed size. Once you create a tuple, you can't change the number of elements it contains. For example, {1, 2, 3} is a tuple with three elements.
- Maps: Maps are collections of key-value pairs. They allow you to associate a value with a specific key. For example, %{name: "Alice", age: 30} is a map where "name" is a key associated with the value "Alice", and "age" is a key associated with the value 30.

Operators

Elixir provides a range of operators to perform operations on data. These include:

- Arithmetic Operators: For performing mathematical calculations, like + (addition), - (subtraction), * (multiplication), and / (division).
- Comparison Operators: For comparing values, like == (equals), != (not equals), > (greater than), and < (less than).
- Logical Operators: For combining boolean values, like and, or, and not.
- String Concatenation: The <> operator is used to join strings together.

Example:

```elixir
# Calculate the area of a circle

radius = 5

pi = 3.14159

area = pi * radius * radius

# Check if a number is even

number = 10

is_even = rem(number, 2) == 0

# Combine strings to create a message

greeting = "Hello, " <> "Elixir!"
```

As you can see, Elixir's syntax and data types are quite straightforward. With a little practice, you'll be able to express your ideas and build complex programs with ease. Remember, the key is to start with the basics and gradually build your understanding.

2.2 Functional Programming Concepts

Elixir is a functional programming language through and through, so understanding these concepts is key to unlocking its full potential. Let's break it down in a way that's easy to grasp, even if you're new to this style of programming.

Functions

In functional programming, functions are treated as first-class citizens. Think of them as the stars of the show! They're not just chunks of code that perform actions; they can be assigned to variables, passed around as arguments to other functions, and even returned as results from functions. This gives you incredible flexibility and power when composing your code.

Let's see this in action:

```Elixir
# Define a function that doubles a number

double = fn (number) -> number * 2 end

# Call the function

result = double.(10) # result will be 20

# Pass the function as an argument to another function

apply_function = fn (function, value) -> function.(value) end

result2 = apply_function.(double, 5) # result2 will be 10
```

As you can see, we can treat functions like any other data type, making our code more modular and reusable.

Immutability

One of the core principles of functional programming is immutability. This means that once you create a piece of data, you can't change it. It might seem strange at first, but this has profound implications for how you write code.

Think of it like this: instead of modifying existing data, you create new data based on the old data. This might sound inefficient, but Elixir is optimized for this approach, and it brings significant benefits:

- Predictability: You can be confident that a variable's value won't change unexpectedly, making your code easier to reason about.
- Concurrency: Immutable data can be safely shared between concurrent processes without the risk of race conditions (where multiple processes try to modify the same data simultaneously).
- Debugging: It's easier to track down bugs when you know that data isn't being modified in unexpected ways.

Let's illustrate this with an example:

```elixir
Elixir

# Create a list

my_list = [1, 2, 3]

# Add an element to the list (this creates a new list)

new_list = [0 | my_list] # new_list will be [0, 1, 2, 3]
```

```
# The original list remains unchanged
IO.inspect(my_list) # Output: [1, 2, 3]
```

Pattern Matching

Pattern matching is a powerful technique in Elixir that allows you to match data against specific patterns and extract values. It's like a sophisticated "if" statement, but much more concise and expressive.

Here's an example:

Elixir

```elixir
# Define a function that greets people differently based on their name
greet = fn
  (:alice) -> "Hello, Alice!"
  (:bob) -> "Hi, Bob!"
  (name) -> "Hello, #{name}!"
end

IO.puts(greet.(:alice))   # Output: Hello, Alice!
IO.puts(greet.(:bob))     # Output: Hi, Bob!
IO.puts(greet.(:carol))   # Output: Hello, Carol!
```

In this example, the greet function uses pattern matching to match the input against different atoms and provide specific greetings.

Recursion

In functional programming, we often use recursion instead of traditional loops. Recursion is a technique where a function calls itself. It might sound a bit mind-bending, but it's a powerful way to solve problems.

Here's a simple example of a recursive function that calculates the factorial of a number:

Elixir

```
defmodule Factorial do

  def of(0), do: 1

  def of(n) when n > 0, do: n * of(n - 1)

end

IO.puts(Factorial.of(5)) # Output: 120
```

Higher-Order Functions: Functions That Operate on Functions

Higher-order functions are functions that take other functions as arguments or return functions as results. They allow you to abstract common patterns and make your code more reusable.

Here's an example:

Elixir

```
# Define a function that applies a function to each element of a list
```

```
map = fn (list, function) ->

  Enum.map(list, function)

end

# Double each element in a list

double_list = map.([1, 2, 3], fn (x) -> x * 2
end) # double_list will be [2, 4, 6]
```

In this example, the map function takes a list and a function as arguments and applies the function to each element of the list.

Functional programming might seem different from what you're used to, but it offers many benefits in terms of code clarity, maintainability, and concurrency. As you become more familiar with Elixir, you'll start to appreciate the elegance and power of this approach.

By embracing immutability, leveraging functions as first-class citizens, and utilizing techniques like pattern matching and recursion, you'll be well-equipped to write robust and efficient Elixir code for your blockchain projects.

2.3 Processes and Concurrency

One of Elixir's most powerful features is its ability to handle concurrency like a champ. You see, in today's world of distributed systems and massive data processing, being able to do multiple things at once is essential. And Elixir, thanks to its roots in Erlang, has concurrency baked right into its core.

Now, you might be familiar with concurrency from other languages, where it often involves threads and locks. But Elixir takes a different approach, one that's more efficient and less prone to errors. Let's explore how Elixir achieves this concurrency magic.

Processes

In Elixir, the fundamental unit of concurrency is the process. Think of a process as a small, independent worker that can execute code concurrently with other processes. But unlike threads, which can be quite resource-intensive, Elixir processes are incredibly lightweight. You can create thousands, even millions, of them without bogging down your system.

This is because Elixir processes are not operating system threads. They are managed by the Erlang virtual machine (BEAM), which provides a highly efficient way to schedule and execute these processes.

Message Passing

So, how do these processes communicate with each other? They do it through message passing. Think of it like sending letters or emails. Each process has a "mailbox" where it can receive messages from other processes. This message passing is asynchronous, meaning that a process can send a message and continue doing other things without waiting for a response.

This approach has several advantages:

- No Shared Memory: Processes don't share memory, which eliminates the risk of race conditions (where multiple processes try to modify the same data simultaneously).
- Isolation: If one process crashes, it doesn't affect other processes, making the system more robust.
- Flexibility: Processes can be located on different machines, enabling distributed computing.

Let's see this in action with a simple example:

```elixir
Elixir

# Spawn a new process that receives a message and prints it

pid = spawn(fn ->

  receive do

    message -> IO.puts("Received message: #{message}")

  end

end)

# Send a message to the process

send(pid, "Hello from another process!")
```

In this code, we first use spawn to create a new process. This process waits for a message using receive. The main process then uses send to deliver a message to the spawned process's mailbox. The spawned process receives the message and prints it to the console.

Real-World Example:

Let's say you're building a chat application. Each user's chat session could be handled by a separate Elixir process. When a user sends a message, their process sends a message to the recipient's process. This allows the application to handle many concurrent chat sessions without slowing down.

Concurrency in Blockchain

In the context of blockchain, concurrency is crucial for handling multiple transactions, validating blocks, and communicating with other nodes in the network. Elixir's lightweight processes and efficient message passing make it well-suited for these tasks.

For example, you could use separate processes to handle:

- Transaction Processing: Validating and processing incoming transactions.
- Block Creation: Creating new blocks and adding them to the blockchain.
- Network Communication: Communicating with other nodes in the network.

Elixir also leverages parallelism, which is the ability to execute multiple tasks simultaneously on different cores of a processor. This is different from concurrency, which focuses on managing multiple tasks over time.

Elixir's ability to utilize multiple cores allows you to further boost the performance of your blockchain applications, especially for computationally intensive tasks like cryptographic operations.

By mastering Elixir's concurrency model, you'll be able to build blockchain applications that are highly performant, scalable, and capable of handling the demands of a distributed network.

2.4 OTP (Open Telecom Platform)

Let's talk about OTP, or Open Telecom Platform. I know the name might sound a bit old-school and telecom-specific, but don't let that fool you. OTP is a powerful set of tools and libraries that lies at the heart of Elixir's robustness and fault-tolerance. It's like the secret sauce that makes Elixir applications incredibly reliable and able to handle unexpected errors with grace.

Think of OTP as a framework for building applications that are designed to run forever. It provides a set of battle-tested abstractions and patterns for managing processes, handling state, and ensuring that your application can recover from failures without missing a beat.

The Three Pillars of OTP

OTP revolves around three core concepts:

1. Supervisors: These are like the guardians of your application. They monitor other processes and ensure that they're running smoothly. If a process crashes, the supervisor can automatically restart it, preventing your application from grinding to a halt.
2. GenServers: GenServer stands for "Generic Server." It's a behavioral module that provides a standard way to build processes that handle state and respond to

requests. Think of it like a blueprint for creating processes that can store data and perform actions based on incoming messages.
3. Applications: OTP provides a way to organize your code into applications, which are essentially self-contained units with their own supervision trees. This helps you structure your code and manage dependencies effectively.

Supervisors

Supervisors are the backbone of OTP's fault-tolerance. They work by organizing processes into a supervision tree. At the top of the tree is a root supervisor, which oversees other supervisors, which in turn oversee worker processes.

This hierarchical structure allows for fine-grained control over how processes are restarted in case of failures. For example, if a worker process crashes, its supervisor can restart it. If the supervisor itself crashes, its parent supervisor can restart it, and so on.

This ensures that your application can recover from errors in a controlled and predictable manner, minimizing downtime and preventing cascading failures.

GenServers: The State Managers

GenServers provide a standardized way to build processes that handle state and respond to requests. They encapsulate state and provide a set of functions for accessing and modifying that state.

Here's a simplified example of a GenServer that keeps track of a counter:

```elixir
defmodule Counter do
  use GenServer

  def start_link(initial_value) do
    GenServer.start_link(__MODULE__, initial_value, name: __MODULE__)[1]
  end

  def increment do
    GenServer.cast(__MODULE__, :increment)
  end

  def value do
    GenServer.call(__MODULE__, :value)
  end

  ## GenServer callbacks
  def init(value) do
    {:ok, value}
  end

  def handle_cast(:increment, state) do
    {:noreply, state + 1}
```

```
  end

  def handle_call(:value, _from, state) do
    {:reply, state, state}
  end
end
```

In this example, the Counter GenServer stores a counter value in its state. It provides functions for incrementing the counter (increment) and retrieving its current value (value).

Applications

OTP applications provide a way to structure your code into modular units. Each application has its own supervision tree, configuration, and dependencies. This helps you manage complex projects and ensure that different parts of your application can be started and stopped independently.

Real-World Example:

Imagine you're building a blockchain node. You could use OTP to structure your node into different applications, such as:

- Network Application: Handles communication with other nodes in the network.
- Transaction Application: Processes and validates transactions.
- Block Creation Application: Creates new blocks and adds them to the blockchain.

Each of these applications would have its own supervision tree, ensuring that the node can recover from errors in any of these components.

OTP's focus on fault-tolerance and concurrency makes it an ideal framework for building blockchain applications. By leveraging OTP's tools and patterns, you can create blockchain nodes and applications that are robust, reliable, and capable of running 24/7.

As you progress through this book, you'll see how OTP plays a crucial role in building real-world blockchain solutions with Elixir.

2.5 Error Handling and Fault Tolerance

There is something that no programmer can avoid: errors. We all make mistakes, and our code is no exception. But in the world of blockchain, where reliability and uptime are paramount, we need to be extra careful about how we handle errors. Fortunately, Elixir provides a robust set of tools and a unique philosophy for dealing with those inevitable hiccups in our code.

The "Let it Crash" Philosophy

Elixir embraces a "let it crash" philosophy. Now, before you start picturing your blockchain application crashing and burning, let me explain. This philosophy isn't about ignoring errors or letting your application run amok. Instead, it's about isolating failures and recovering from them gracefully.

Think of it like this: instead of trying to prevent every possible error, which can be an impossible task, you design your system to handle failures in a controlled manner. When an error occurs, you let the affected part of the system crash, but you contain the damage and allow the rest of the system to continue functioning.

This might seem counterintuitive, but it actually leads to more robust and reliable applications. By isolating failures, you prevent them from cascading through your system and causing widespread damage.

Error Handling Mechanisms

Elixir provides several mechanisms for handling errors:

- **try...catch** Blocks: These allow you to wrap potentially error-prone code and handle exceptions if they occur.

```Elixir
try do
  # Code that might raise an error
  result = 10 / 0
catch
  ArithmeticError -> IO.puts("Cannot divide by zero!")
end
```

- **with Statement**: This provides a more concise way to handle errors, especially when dealing with multiple function calls that might return errors.

```Elixir
with {:ok, file} <- File.open("my_file.txt"),
     {:ok, content} <- File.read(file) do
  IO.puts("File content: #{content}")
else
  {:error, reason} -> IO.puts("Error reading file: #{reason}")
end
```

- **raise and throw**: These allow you to raise exceptions explicitly when you encounter an error condition.

```Elixir
defmodule MyModule do
  def my_function(value) when value < 0 do
    raise "Value cannot be negative"
  end
end
```

OTP and Fault Tolerance

OTP (Open Telecom Platform), which we discussed in the previous section, plays a crucial role in Elixir's fault-tolerance. OTP supervisors monitor processes and restart them if they crash, ensuring that your application remains stable.

This is particularly important in blockchain applications, where nodes need to be constantly running to maintain the integrity of the network. By using OTP supervisors, you can ensure that your blockchain nodes can recover from errors and continue operating without interruption.

Real-World Example:

Let's say you're building a blockchain node that receives transactions from other nodes. If an error occurs while processing a transaction, you could use a `try...catch` block to catch the error and log it. You could then use an OTP supervisor to restart the process, ensuring that the node can continue receiving and processing other transactions.

Importance of Logging and Monitoring

While Elixir provides excellent tools for handling errors, it's also important to log errors and monitor your application for potential issues. This allows you to identify and address problems proactively, preventing them from escalating into major incidents.

By combining Elixir's error handling mechanisms with OTP's fault-tolerance capabilities, you can build blockchain applications that are robust, resilient, and capable of handling the challenges of a distributed and ever-changing environment.

Chapter 3: Smart Contracts with Elixir

Think of smart contracts as self-executing agreements written in code. They automatically enforce the terms of a contract without the need for intermediaries or manual intervention. It's like having a digital lawyer built right into the blockchain.

Now, you might be wondering, "How do smart contracts fit into the picture with Elixir?" Well, that's exactly what we're going to explore in this chapter. We'll look at what smart contracts are, how they work, and how Elixir can play a role in their development.

3.1 Understanding Smart Contracts

Smart contracts are simply programs that automatically execute on a blockchain when certain conditions are met. Think of them as self-enforcing agreements written in code.

Traditional Contracts vs. Smart Contracts

Let's make a comparison to traditional contracts. Say you're renting an apartment. You and your landlord sign a lease agreement that outlines the terms: monthly rent, lease duration, and so on. This contract is enforced by legal systems and relies on trust between you and the landlord.

Now, imagine a similar agreement, but instead of a paper document, it's a smart contract on a blockchain. This contract could automatically deduct the rent from your account and transfer it to the landlord's account each month. No more manual payments or worries about late fees!

Key Characteristics of Smart Contracts

- Self-Executing: They automatically enforce the terms of the contract without the need for intermediaries or manual intervention.
- Immutable: Once deployed to a blockchain, they cannot be altered or tampered with, ensuring the integrity of the agreement.
- Transparent: The code and execution of the contract are visible to all participants, promoting accountability and trust.
- Decentralized: They are not controlled by a single entity, making them resistant to censorship and single points of failure.

Breaking Down the Mechanics

Let's take a closer look at how smart contracts actually work:

1. Writing the Contract: Smart contracts are written in specialized programming languages (more on that later). The code defines the rules and logic of the agreement.
2. Deployment: The contract is compiled into bytecode and deployed to a blockchain platform that supports smart contracts, like Ethereum.

3. Triggering the Contract: When a specific condition defined in the contract is met (e.g., a certain date arrives, a payment is received), the contract is triggered.
4. Execution: The blockchain network executes the contract's code. This execution might involve transferring funds, updating data on the blockchain, or interacting with other smart contracts.

Illustrative Example

Let's say you're creating a decentralized escrow service. You could write a smart contract that:

- Holds funds in escrow until both the buyer and seller fulfill their obligations.
- Automatically releases the funds to the seller once the buyer confirms receipt of the goods.
- Refunds the buyer if the seller fails to deliver the goods within a specified timeframe.

This eliminates the need for a trusted third party to manage the escrow process, reducing costs and increasing efficiency.

Real-World Applications

Smart contracts are already being used in a variety of ways:

- Decentralized Finance (DeFi): Creating decentralized lending platforms, exchanges, and other financial instruments.
- Supply Chain Management: Tracking goods and products, automating payments, and ensuring ethical sourcing.

- Digital Identity: Managing and verifying digital identities, granting access to services based on predefined conditions.
- Gaming: Creating in-game assets and economies, managing ownership and transactions.

Benefits in Action

Let's consider a real-world example: a supply chain tracking system for coffee beans. A smart contract could be used to:

- Record the origin and journey of the coffee beans, from farm to roastery.
- Automatically release payments to farmers upon delivery of the beans.
- Track the sustainability certifications of the coffee, ensuring ethical sourcing.

This provides transparency and accountability throughout the supply chain, benefiting both consumers and producers.

By understanding the core concepts of smart contracts, you can start to appreciate their potential to revolutionize how we interact and do business in a digital world. In the next section, we'll explore the languages used to write these powerful agreements.

3.2 Smart Contract Languages

Now that you have a good grasp of what smart contracts are, let's talk about the languages we use to write them. You see, just like we use different languages to communicate with people from different parts of the world, we use different languages to write smart contracts for different blockchain platforms.

These languages are specifically designed to be secure, reliable, and suitable for the unique environment of a blockchain. Let's explore some of the most popular ones:

1. Solidity

If you're interested in writing smart contracts for Ethereum, the most popular blockchain platform for smart contracts, then Solidity is your go-to language. It was specifically created for Ethereum and has become the dominant language in the smart contract world.

Think of Solidity as the JavaScript of Ethereum. It's a high-level language with a syntax that resembles JavaScript and C++. This makes it relatively easy to learn, especially if you have experience with those languages.

Here's a simple example of a Solidity contract:

```solidity
Solidity

pragma solidity ^0.8.0;

contract Greeter {

    string public greeting;

    constructor(string memory _greeting) {

        greeting = _greeting;

    }
```

```
    function greet() public view returns (string¹
memory) {

        return greeting;²

    }

}
```

This contract defines a simple "Greeter" that stores a greeting message and has a function to retrieve it.

Key Features of Solidity:

- Statically Typed: Helps catch errors early in the development process.
- Object-Oriented: Supports concepts like contracts, inheritance, and libraries.
- Turing-Complete: Can theoretically perform any computation, making it highly versatile.

2. Vyper

Vyper is another popular language for writing smart contracts on Ethereum. It was designed with a focus on security, auditability, and simplicity.

Vyper's syntax is inspired by Python, making it easy to read and understand. It also intentionally omits some features of Solidity that can lead to security vulnerabilities, such as modifiers and inline assembly.

Here's an example of a Vyper contract:

```
Code snippet

# @version ^0.3.1
```

```
greeting: public(String[100])

@external

def __init__(_greeting: String[100]):

    self.greeting = _greeting

@external

@view

def greet() -> String[100]:

    return self.greeting
```

This contract is similar to the Solidity example, but with a more Pythonic syntax.

Key Features of Vyper:

- Security-Focused: Designed to prevent common security vulnerabilities.
- Auditability: Easier to audit and verify due to its simpler syntax and restricted features.
- Pythonic Syntax: Familiar to Python developers.

3. Rust

While Solidity and Vyper are the most popular choices for Ethereum, other blockchain platforms support different languages. For example, Polkadot and Solana use Rust for their smart contracts.

Rust is a systems programming language known for its performance, safety, and memory efficiency. It's a more complex language to learn than Solidity or Vyper, but its focus on safety and performance makes it a good choice for writing critical smart contracts.

Choosing the Right Language

The best language for your smart contract project depends on several factors:

- Blockchain Platform: The platform you're targeting will often dictate the language you need to use.
- Project Requirements: Consider the complexity of your contract, performance requirements, and security concerns.
- Developer Experience: Choose a language that you're comfortable with or willing to learn.

While Elixir might not be the most common choice for writing smart contracts directly on popular platforms like Ethereum, it can still play a valuable role in the broader ecosystem. You can use Elixir to build applications that interact with smart contracts, provide user interfaces, or even create your own blockchain platforms that support Elixir-based smart contracts.

As you continue your journey into the world of blockchain and smart contracts, remember that the language you choose is just one piece of the puzzle. The most important thing is to understand the underlying concepts and security considerations to build robust and reliable decentralized applications.

3.3 Elixir and Smart Contracts

Let's address the big question now: "Can I write smart contracts with Elixir?" The answer, as with many things in technology, is nuanced. While Elixir isn't the most common choice for writing smart contracts *directly* on established platforms like Ethereum, it's far from excluded from this exciting space. Let's explore the possibilities and how Elixir can contribute to the smart contract ecosystem.

The Challenge with Established Platforms

The main hurdle is that popular smart contract platforms like Ethereum have their own virtual machines (EVM) and preferred languages (like Solidity and Vyper). Elixir doesn't natively compile to bytecode that runs directly on the EVM.

Think of it like trying to run a Windows program on a Mac without an emulator. The underlying architectures are different, and you need a bridge to translate between them.

Bridging the Gap: WebAssembly (WASM)

However, there's a rising star in the world of portable code: WebAssembly (WASM). WASM is a low-level bytecode format designed to be efficient and portable across different environments, including blockchain virtual machines.

And guess what? You can compile Elixir code to WASM! This opens up exciting possibilities for running Elixir-based smart contracts on platforms that support WASM.

Here's a simplified illustration:

1. Write your smart contract logic in Elixir.
2. Use a toolchain to compile your Elixir code to WASM.
3. Deploy the WASM bytecode to a blockchain platform that supports WASM execution.

While this approach is still relatively new, it's gaining traction, and we can expect to see more blockchain platforms embracing WASM in the future.

Elixir's Strengths: Off-Chain and Interoperability

Even if direct on-chain execution with Elixir isn't always the primary route, remember Elixir's strengths:

- Concurrency: Perfect for building highly concurrent systems that can handle the demands of interacting with a blockchain.
- Fault Tolerance: Ensures your applications can recover from errors gracefully, crucial for interacting with a decentralized network.
- Scalability: Handles a growing number of users and transactions efficiently.

These strengths make Elixir a fantastic choice for building the *surrounding infrastructure* of smart contracts:

- Off-Chain Logic: Handle complex business logic, data processing, and user interactions off-chain in your Elixir applications.
- Interoperability: Use Elixir to build APIs and interfaces that interact with smart contracts written in other languages.
- Blockchain Explorers and Tools: Create tools and explorers to monitor and analyze blockchain data.

Real-World Example:

Imagine a decentralized marketplace built on Ethereum. You could use Solidity to write the core smart contracts that handle the buying and selling of goods. But you could use Elixir to build:

- A user-friendly web interface for interacting with the marketplace.
- An API that allows other applications to access the marketplace's functionality.
- A backend system that processes orders and manages user data.

This allows you to leverage the strengths of both Solidity and Elixir to create a robust and efficient decentralized application.

Alternative Blockchains and the Future

It's worth noting that some blockchain platforms are exploring or have implemented support for Elixir or Erlang-based smart contracts. This could lead to more direct integration of Elixir in the smart contract space.

As the blockchain ecosystem evolves, we can expect to see more innovation and experimentation with different languages and approaches. Elixir, with its strong foundation and growing community, is well-positioned to play a significant role in this exciting future.

By understanding the different ways Elixir can interact with smart contracts, you can leverage its strengths to build robust, scalable, and secure decentralized applications. Whether you're building off-chain logic, interacting with existing contracts, or exploring new platforms, Elixir offers a powerful toolkit for blockchain development.

3.4 Security Considerations for Smart Contracts

Let's talk about the security of smart contracts: You see, smart contracts are pieces of code that execute on a blockchain, and like any code, they can have bugs or vulnerabilities. But here's the catch: once a smart contract is deployed to a blockchain, it's incredibly difficult, if not impossible, to change.

This means that any security flaws can have serious consequences, potentially leading to loss of funds, data breaches, or even the complete failure of your decentralized application. So, it's absolutely crucial to prioritize security throughout the entire smart contract development lifecycle.

Think of it like building a bank vault. You wouldn't want to leave any gaps or weaknesses in its design, right? Similarly, you need to be meticulous when writing and deploying smart contracts.

Common Security Vulnerabilities

Let's take a look at some common security vulnerabilities that can plague smart contracts:

- Reentrancy Attacks: These occur when a malicious contract repeatedly calls a vulnerable contract's function before the first call is completed, potentially draining funds.
- Integer Overflows and Underflows: These happen when arithmetic operations result in values that

exceed the maximum or minimum values that a variable can hold, leading to unexpected behavior.
- Logic Errors: Flaws in the contract's logic can lead to unintended consequences, such as allowing unauthorized access or incorrect calculations.
- Denial of Service (DoS) Attacks: Attackers can overload a contract with requests, preventing legitimate users from accessing it.

Best Practices for Secure Smart Contracts

Now, don't let these vulnerabilities scare you off! There are many things you can do to secure your smart contracts:

1. Code Audits: Think of this like having a professional inspector examine your bank vault. Code audits involve having experienced security experts review your smart contract code to identify potential vulnerabilities. This is a crucial step in ensuring the security of your contract.
2. Formal Verification: This is a more advanced technique that uses mathematical methods to prove the correctness of your contract's logic. It's like having a mathematical guarantee that your contract behaves as intended.
3. Thorough Testing: Just like with any software, testing is crucial. Test your smart contract with various inputs and scenarios to ensure it behaves as expected and handles edge cases correctly.
4. Secure Coding Practices: Follow secure coding practices to prevent common vulnerabilities. This includes using well-established libraries, avoiding complex logic, and validating inputs carefully.

5. Keep it Simple: Avoid unnecessary complexity in your contracts. The simpler the code, the easier it is to audit and understand, reducing the risk of errors.
6. Consider Upgradability: While immutability is a key feature of blockchains, you might need to upgrade your contract in the future to fix bugs or add new features. Consider using techniques like proxy patterns to allow for upgradability without compromising security.

Real-World Example:

The DAO (Decentralized Autonomous Organization) hack in 2016 is a prime example of what can go wrong when smart contract security is overlooked. A vulnerability in the DAO's code allowed an attacker to drain millions of dollars worth of Ether. This incident highlighted the importance of thorough security audits and testing.

Remember, security is not a one-time task. It's an ongoing process that requires constant vigilance. Stay up-to-date on the latest security best practices, vulnerabilities, and attack vectors. The blockchain ecosystem is constantly evolving, and new threats can emerge at any time.

By prioritizing security and following best practices, you can build smart contracts that are robust, reliable, and resistant to attacks. This will ensure the success of your decentralized applications and protect the interests of your users.

Chapter 4: Data Structures and Algorithms for Blockchain

It's time to peek under the hood and explore the inner workings of blockchain technology! While we've discussed the general concepts, understanding the specific data structures and algorithms that make it all tick is crucial for building robust and efficient blockchain applications.

Think of it like learning about the engine of a car. You might know how to drive, but understanding how the engine works allows you to appreciate its power and diagnose problems more effectively.

4.1 Hashing Algorithms

Hashing is like a magic trick that takes data of any size – a sentence, a book, an entire movie – and transforms it into a unique, fixed-size code called a hash. Think of it as a digital fingerprint for your data.

Now, you might be wondering, "Why is this so important for blockchain?" Well, hashes play a crucial role in ensuring the integrity and security of the blockchain. Let me explain how.

The beauty of hashing algorithms is that they produce unique hashes for different inputs. Even a tiny change in the input data, like changing a single letter in a sentence, will result in a completely different hash. This property is essential for maintaining the integrity of the blockchain.

Ensuring Data Integrity

In a blockchain, each block of data contains a hash of its contents. This hash acts like a seal, guaranteeing that the data hasn't been tampered with. If someone tries to modify even a single bit of information in the block, the hash will change, alerting the network to a potential problem.

This is like having a tamper-evident seal on a product. If the seal is broken, you know that someone might have messed with the contents.

Linking Blocks Together

Hashes are also used to link blocks together in a chain. Each block contains not only the hash of its own data but also the hash of the previous block. This creates a chain of blocks, where each block is linked to the one before it.

This linking mechanism is crucial for the immutability of the blockchain. If someone tries to alter a block in the middle of the chain, it would change the hash of that block, which would then affect the hash of the next block, and so on, all the way to the end of the chain. This would make the tampering attempt immediately obvious to everyone on the network.

Efficient Data Retrieval

Hashes also play a role in efficient data retrieval. Instead of searching through the entire blockchain for a specific piece of information, you can use the hash to directly access the relevant block. This is like having a library catalog that allows you to quickly locate a book based on its unique call number.

Popular Hashing Algorithms in Blockchain

There are several hashing algorithms commonly used in blockchain technology:

- SHA-256: This is the most widely used hashing algorithm in blockchain. It's used in Bitcoin and many other cryptocurrencies. SHA-256 produces a 256-bit hash, which is a string of 64 hexadecimal characters.
- SHA-3: This is a more recent hashing algorithm that offers improved security and performance compared to SHA-256.
- Keccak-256: This is a variant of SHA-3 that's used in Ethereum.

Hashing in Action: An Elixir Example

Let's see how you can calculate a hash in Elixir using the :crypto module:

```
Elixir

iex> :crypto.hash(:sha256, "This is a test string")
<<198, 146, 185, 207, 166, 68, 123, 114, 137, 19, 221, 174, 101, 113, 15, 131,
  107, 235, 108, 161, 187, 208, 119, 171, 232, 140, 103, 147, 16, 112, 249, 145>>
```

This code snippet calculates the SHA-256 hash of the string "This is a test string". Try changing even a single character in the string, and you'll see that the resulting hash is completely different.

Real-World Example:

In Bitcoin, each transaction is hashed, and these transaction hashes are then organized into a Merkle tree (which we'll discuss in the next section). The Merkle root, which is the hash at the top of the tree, is included in the block header. This allows anyone to verify the integrity of all transactions in the block by checking only the Merkle root.

By understanding the role of hashing algorithms in blockchain, you can appreciate how they contribute to the security, immutability, and efficiency of this revolutionary technology.

4.2 Merkle Trees

Another data structure that plays a crucial role in blockchain technology: Merkle trees. Now, the name might sound a bit intimidating, but trust me, the concept is quite straightforward. Think of a Merkle tree as a clever way to organize and verify data, kind of like a pyramid where each level builds upon the one below it.

Building the Pyramid

At the base of the Merkle tree are the individual pieces of data, like transactions in a blockchain. Each pair of data elements is then hashed together, and these resulting hashes are paired and hashed again, and so on. This process continues until you reach the top of the pyramid, where a single hash, called the Merkle root, represents the entire set of data.

Why Are Merkle Trees So Useful in Blockchain?

- Efficient Verification: Let's say you want to verify that a specific transaction is included in a block. With a Merkle tree, you don't need to check every single transaction in the block. You only need to check a small path of hashes leading from the transaction to the Merkle root. This significantly reduces the amount of data you need to process.
- Data Integrity: Since each hash in the Merkle tree depends on the hashes below it, any change to the data, even a tiny one, will propagate up the tree and ultimately change the Merkle root. This makes it incredibly difficult to tamper with the data without being detected.
- Space Efficiency: Merkle trees allow for a compact representation of a large set of data. Instead of storing all the individual data elements, you can simply store the Merkle root, which acts as a summary of the entire dataset.

Let's illustrate this with an example:

Suppose we have four transactions in a block: A, B, C, and D.

1. Hash each transaction: We calculate the hash of each transaction individually: Hash(A), Hash(B), Hash(C), and Hash(D).

2. Pair and hash: We pair the transaction hashes and hash them together: Hash(Hash(A) + Hash(B)) and Hash(Hash(C) + Hash(D)).
3. Hash again: We hash the resulting hashes together to get the Merkle root: Hash(Hash(Hash(A) + Hash(B)) + Hash(Hash(C) + Hash(D))).

Now, if we want to verify that transaction C is included in the block, we only need to check the following hashes:

- Hash(C)
- Hash(Hash(C) + Hash(D))
- Hash(Hash(Hash(A) + Hash(B)) + Hash(Hash(C) + Hash(D))) (the Merkle root)

Real-World Example:

Bitcoin uses Merkle trees to efficiently verify transactions within a block. The Merkle root is included in the block header, which is a small summary of the block's contents. When a node receives a new block, it can verify the integrity of all transactions in the block by checking only the Merkle root and a small number of hashes.

Merkle Trees in Elixir

While Elixir doesn't have a built-in Merkle tree implementation in its standard library, there are several third-party libraries available that provide this functionality. You can use these libraries to create and manipulate Merkle trees in your Elixir blockchain applications.

Example using the :crypto **module and list comprehensions:**

```elixir
defmodule MyMerkleTree do
  def hash(data) do
    :crypto.hash(:sha256, data)
  end

  def build(transactions) do
    hashes = Enum.map(transactions, &hash/1)
    build_tree(hashes)
  end

  defp build_tree(hashes) when length(hashes) == 1 do
    hd(hashes)
  end

  defp build_tree(hashes) do
    paired_hashes = Enum.chunk_every(hashes, 2, 2, :duplicate)
    next_level_hashes = for {h1, h2} <- paired_hashes, do: hash(h1 <> h2)
    build_tree(next_level_hashes)
  end
```

```
end

transactions = ["A", "B", "C", "D"]

merkle_root = MyMerkleTree.build(transactions)

IO.inspect(merkle_root)
```

This example demonstrates a basic Merkle tree implementation in Elixir. The build function takes a list of transactions, hashes each transaction, and then recursively builds the Merkle tree by pairing and hashing the hashes until a single Merkle root is obtained.

Understanding Merkle trees, you gain a deeper appreciation for the ingenuity behind blockchain technology and how it achieves efficiency and security in data management.

4.3 Cryptographic Signatures and Digital Wallets

Cryptographic signatures and digital wallets are essential for understanding how ownership and authenticity are established in the world of cryptocurrencies and decentralized applications.

Cryptographic Signatures

Think of a cryptographic signature as a digital equivalent of a handwritten signature. It allows you to verify the authenticity and integrity of a message or transaction. In the context of blockchain, it's used to prove that a particular transaction originated from a specific user and hasn't been tampered with.

How do these digital signatures work?

They rely on a clever technique called public-key cryptography. In this system, each user has a pair of keys:

- Private Key: This key is like your secret password. You keep it safe and never share it with anyone.
- Public Key: This key is like your public email address. You can share it with anyone who needs to verify your signature.

Now, let's say you want to send some cryptocurrency to a friend. Here's how the signature process works:

1. Create a Transaction: You create a transaction message that specifies the amount of cryptocurrency you want to send and your friend's public key (their "address").
2. Sign the Transaction: You use your private key to generate a unique digital signature for the transaction. This signature is like a tamper-proof seal that proves the transaction came from you.
3. Broadcast the Transaction: You broadcast the signed transaction to the blockchain network.
4. Verification: Other nodes on the network receive your transaction and use your public key to verify the signature. If the signature is valid, they know that the transaction indeed came from you and hasn't been altered.

The beauty of this system is that you never have to share your private key with anyone. The public key is enough to verify your signature, ensuring that only you can authorize transactions from your account.

Digital Wallets: Your Secure Vault

Now, where do you store these important keys? That's where digital wallets come in. Think of a digital wallet as a secure container for your private keys. It's like your personal bank vault for managing your cryptocurrencies.

Digital wallets come in various forms:

- Software Wallets: These are applications that you install on your computer or mobile device.
- Hardware Wallets: These are physical devices that store your private keys offline, providing an extra layer of security.
- Paper Wallets: These are simply pieces of paper with your private and public keys printed on them.

The type of wallet you choose depends on your needs and security preferences. If you're just starting out, a software wallet might be sufficient. But if you're dealing with large amounts of cryptocurrency, a hardware wallet is generally recommended for its enhanced security.

Real-World Example:

When you use a cryptocurrency exchange like Coinbase or Binance, you're essentially interacting with their digital wallets. When you deposit cryptocurrency into the exchange, you're transferring it to their wallet. When you withdraw, they're sending it from their wallet to yours.

Elixir and Digital Wallets

While Elixir doesn't have built-in functionality for managing digital wallets, you can use it to build applications that interact with wallets and blockchain networks. For example, you could use Elixir to:

- Create a wallet service: Build a backend service that manages users' wallets and allows them to send and receive cryptocurrency.
- Develop a blockchain explorer: Create a tool that allows users to view transactions, balances, and other blockchain data.
- Build a decentralized application (DApp): Develop a DApp that interacts with a blockchain and allows users to manage their digital assets.

Code Example (Conceptual):

```elixir
# This is a simplified example, actual cryptographic operations are more complex

defmodule Wallet do

  def generate_key_pair do
    # Use a cryptographic library to generate a key pair
    {:ok, private_key, public_key} = Crypto.generate_key_pair()

    %{private_key: private_key, public_key: public_key}

  end

  def sign_transaction(transaction, private_key) do
```

```
    # Use a cryptographic library to sign the transaction
    signature = Crypto.sign(transaction, private_key)

    %{transaction: transaction, signature: signature}
  end

  def verify_signature(transaction, signature, public_key) do
    # Use a cryptographic library to verify the signature
    Crypto.verify(transaction, signature, public_key)
  end
end
```

This example demonstrates a simplified implementation of generating key pairs, signing transactions, and verifying signatures. In a real-world scenario, you would use a robust cryptographic library like :crypto or a third-party library for these operations.

Understanding cryptographic signatures and digital wallets, you gain a deeper understanding of how ownership and security are managed in the blockchain world. This knowledge will be invaluable as you build your own blockchain applications with Elixir.

4.4 Efficient Data Handling in Blockchain

As blockchain networks grow and more transactions are recorded, the amount of data stored on the blockchain can become massive. This can lead to challenges with storage, scalability, and performance.

Think of it like a library. If the library keeps adding books without any organization or efficient storage system, it becomes harder and harder to find what you're looking for, and the building might eventually run out of space!

Similarly, in blockchain, if we don't handle data efficiently, it can lead to slower transaction processing, increased storage costs, and even network congestion.

Strategies for Efficient Data Handling

Fortunately, there are several strategies and techniques used to address these challenges:

1. Data Pruning

One approach is to prune, or remove, old or unnecessary data from the blockchain. This is like decluttering your house – getting rid of things you no longer need to free up space.

In blockchain, data pruning can involve removing old transaction data that is no longer relevant or storing only a summary of the data instead of the full details. This can significantly reduce the storage requirements for nodes on the network.

2. State Channels

State channels are like creating a separate "room" outside the main blockchain to handle certain transactions. They allow participants to conduct multiple transactions off-chain without needing to record each transaction on the main blockchain.

Think of it like this: you and your friend frequently exchange small amounts of money. Instead of recording each transaction on the main blockchain, you could open a state channel, conduct your transactions off-chain, and then settle the final balance on the main blockchain later.

This reduces the load on the main blockchain and allows for faster and cheaper transactions.

3. Sharding

Sharding is like dividing the blockchain into smaller, more manageable pieces called shards. Each shard handles a portion of the network's transactions and data. This is similar to how a large company might have different departments handling different aspects of the business.

Sharding improves scalability by distributing the workload across multiple shards, allowing the network to handle a larger number of transactions.

4. Efficient Data Structures

Using efficient data structures, like the Merkle trees we discussed earlier, can also help optimize data storage and retrieval. Merkle trees allow for compact representation of data and efficient verification, reducing storage needs and improving performance.

5. Compression Techniques

Just like we compress files on our computers to save space, compression techniques can be applied to blockchain data to reduce its size. This can involve using algorithms to compress transaction data or storing data in a more compact format.

Real-World Examples

- Bitcoin: Bitcoin uses a technique called "pruned full nodes" where nodes can choose to discard old blocks of transaction data, keeping only the most recent ones.
- Ethereum: Ethereum is working on implementing sharding to improve its scalability and handle a growing number of transactions.
- Lightning Network: The Lightning Network is a layer-2 scaling solution for Bitcoin that uses state channels to enable faster and cheaper transactions.

Elixir's Role in Efficient Data Handling

Elixir, with its focus on concurrency and fault-tolerance, can play a crucial role in building efficient data handling solutions for blockchain. You can use Elixir to:

- Develop data pruning algorithms: Implement algorithms that efficiently prune old or unnecessary data from the blockchain.
- Build state channel infrastructure: Create the infrastructure for managing and settling state channels.

- Develop sharding solutions: Implement the logic for sharding a blockchain network and managing communication between shards.
- Optimize data storage: Use efficient data structures and compression techniques to optimize data storage and retrieval.

Code Example (Conceptual):

Elixir

```
# This is a simplified example, actual implementations are more complex

defmodule DataPruning do

  def prune_old_blocks(blockchain, threshold) do

    # Filter out blocks older than the threshold

    Enum.filter(blockchain, fn block -> block.timestamp > threshold end)

  end

end
```

This example demonstrates a simple data pruning function that removes blocks older than a certain threshold. In a real-world scenario, you would need to consider various factors like block size, transaction frequency, and storage capacity when implementing data pruning.

By understanding the importance of efficient data handling and the various techniques available, you can build blockchain applications that are scalable, performant, and sustainable in the long run.

Chapter 5: Designing a Blockchain Network

It's time to put on our architect hats and start designing our own blockchain network using the power of Elixir! We've covered the fundamental concepts and building blocks, and now we'll put them together to create a decentralized system that can handle transactions, store data securely, and operate reliably.

Think of this chapter as a blueprint for your blockchain project. We'll explore the key components, design decisions, and considerations that go into creating a robust and efficient blockchain network.

5.1 Blockchain Architecture

Before we get into the nitty-gritty, let's zoom out and look at the overall structure of a blockchain network. At its core, a blockchain is a distributed ledger, meaning the data isn't stored in one central location but is spread across multiple computers, called nodes. These nodes work together to maintain a shared, synchronized copy of the blockchain.

Key Players in the Blockchain Ecosystem

- Nodes: These are the individual computers that participate in the blockchain network. Each node runs blockchain software and stores a copy of the entire blockchain or a portion of it. Think of them as the workers that keep the network running.

- Blocks: These are the containers for data that get added to the blockchain. Each block typically contains a set of transactions, a timestamp, and a link to the previous block in the chain. They're like the pages in a ledger, recording the history of transactions.
- Transactions: These are the individual actions or data exchanges that are recorded on the blockchain. In a cryptocurrency blockchain, a transaction might represent a transfer of funds from one user to another. In a supply chain blockchain, it might represent the movement of goods from a warehouse to a store.
- Consensus Mechanism: This is the magic ingredient that ensures all nodes agree on the state of the blockchain. It's a set of rules that determine how new blocks are added to the chain and how conflicts are resolved. We'll discuss consensus mechanisms in more detail later in this chapter.
- Network Protocol: This defines the rules for how nodes communicate with each other. It specifies how nodes discover each other, exchange information, and maintain connections.

Design Considerations: Building a Solid Foundation

When designing your blockchain architecture, you need to think carefully about several factors:

- Scalability: How many transactions per second (TPS) do you need your blockchain to handle? If you're building a global payment system, you'll need to handle a much higher TPS than a small-scale supply chain tracking system.

- Security: How will you protect your blockchain from attacks and ensure the integrity of the data? This involves using strong cryptographic algorithms, implementing robust consensus mechanisms, and designing secure network protocols.
- Decentralization: How will you ensure that your blockchain is truly decentralized and not controlled by a single entity? This is crucial for maintaining the trust and transparency of the system.
- Performance: How will you optimize your blockchain for speed and efficiency? This might involve using efficient data structures, optimizing network communication, and choosing appropriate hardware.
- Storage: How will you handle the growing amount of data stored on the blockchain? This might involve using data pruning techniques, implementing state channels, or utilizing decentralized storage solutions.

Real-World Example: Bitcoin's Architecture

Let's take a look at Bitcoin's architecture as an example. Bitcoin uses a Proof-of-Work (PoW) consensus mechanism, where miners compete to solve complex mathematical problems to add new blocks to the chain. It uses a peer-to-peer network protocol for communication between nodes. Each node stores a full copy of the blockchain, and transactions are grouped into blocks that are chained together chronologically.

Elixir's Role in Blockchain Architecture

Elixir, with its strengths in concurrency, fault-tolerance, and scalability, is well-suited for building various components of a blockchain network. You can use Elixir to:

- Implement node functionality: Create the logic for nodes to validate transactions, participate in the consensus process, and communicate with other nodes.
- Develop APIs and interfaces: Build APIs that allow external applications to interact with your blockchain.
- Create blockchain explorers and tools: Develop tools for monitoring and analyzing the blockchain data.

By understanding the key components of blockchain architecture and the design considerations involved, you can lay a solid foundation for building your own blockchain network with Elixir.

5.2 Consensus Mechanisms in Elixir

Consensus mechanisms are the ingenious algorithms that ensure all nodes in the network agree on a single version of the truth, even if some nodes are mischievous or malfunctioning. Think of them as the referees that ensure fair play and prevent cheating in the blockchain game.

Why Do We Need Consensus?

In a distributed system like a blockchain, where data is spread across multiple nodes, it's crucial to have a mechanism that guarantees everyone is on the same page. Without consensus, you could have different nodes with conflicting versions of the blockchain, leading to chaos and distrust.

Types of Consensus Mechanisms

There are several popular consensus mechanisms used in blockchain, each with its own strengths and weaknesses:

1. Proof of Work (PoW)

This is the OG consensus mechanism, used by Bitcoin. It's like a competitive race where nodes (called miners in this case) compete to solve complex mathematical problems. The first miner to solve the problem gets to add a new block to the chain and receives a reward.

This process is energy-intensive, but it's also very secure, as it requires a significant amount of computational power to manipulate the blockchain.

2. Proof of Stake (PoS)

This is a more energy-efficient alternative to PoW. Instead of relying on computational power, PoS relies on stake. Nodes that hold a larger amount of cryptocurrency in the network have a higher chance of being selected to add new blocks.

This mechanism is generally faster and more environmentally friendly than PoW, but it can be susceptible to certain types of attacks, such as "nothing at stake" attacks where validators can vote on multiple chains without consequence.

3. Delegated Proof of Stake (DPoS)

This is a variation of PoS where token holders vote for delegates who are responsible for validating transactions and adding blocks to the chain. This is like electing representatives to make decisions on behalf of the community.

DPoS is generally faster and more efficient than PoW and PoS, but it can be less decentralized, as the power is concentrated in the hands of the delegates.

4. Practical Byzantine Fault Tolerance (PBFT)

This is a more complex consensus mechanism that can tolerate a certain number of faulty or malicious nodes. It involves a series of rounds of communication and voting between nodes to reach consensus.

PBFT is highly resilient to failures but can be less scalable than other mechanisms, as the communication overhead increases with the number of nodes.

The choice of consensus mechanism depends on the specific needs and goals of your blockchain. Consider factors like:

- Security: How important is resistance to attacks and manipulation?
- Performance: How fast do you need to process transactions and add blocks?
- Energy Efficiency: How much energy consumption is acceptable?
- Decentralization: How decentralized do you want the network to be?

Implementing Consensus Mechanisms in Elixir

Elixir, with its powerful concurrency model and fault-tolerance features, is well-suited for implementing various consensus mechanisms. You can use Elixir's processes and message passing to simulate the behavior of nodes in a blockchain network and implement the logic for validating transactions and adding blocks.

Example (Conceptual):

```elixir
# This is a simplified example, actual implementations are more complex

defmodule ProofOfWork do

  def mine_block(block, difficulty) do

    # Generate a random nonce

    nonce = :rand.uniform(1000000)

    # Calculate the hash of the block with the nonce

    hash = :crypto.hash(:sha256, block.data <> Integer.to_string(nonce))

    # Check if the hash meets the difficulty requirement

    if hash < difficulty do

      # Block mined successfully!

      %{block | nonce: nonce, hash: hash}
```

```
    else
      # Try again with a different nonce
      mine_block(block, difficulty)
    end
  end
end
```

This example demonstrates a simplified implementation of a Proof-of-Work mining function. In a real-world scenario, you would need to implement more complex logic for difficulty adjustment, block validation, and reward distribution.

Real-World Examples

- Bitcoin: Uses Proof of Work (PoW)
- Ethereum 2.0: Uses Proof of Stake (PoS)
- EOS: Uses Delegated Proof of Stake (DPoS)
- Hyperledger Fabric: Uses Practical Byzantine Fault Tolerance (PBFT)

Understanding the different consensus mechanisms and how to implement them in Elixir, you can design a blockchain network that meets your specific needs and provides a secure and reliable platform for decentralized applications.

5.3 Node Communication and Networking

A blockchain isn't just a bunch of isolated computers; it's a dynamic network where nodes constantly communicate to share information, validate transactions, and keep the blockchain synchronized. Think of it like a bustling city where people interact and exchange goods and services to keep the economy running.

The Peer-to-Peer (P2P) Network

Most blockchains utilize a peer-to-peer (P2P) network architecture. This means that there's no central server controlling the communication. Instead, each node acts as both a client and a server, directly connecting and communicating with other nodes.

This decentralized structure makes the network more resilient to failures and censorship. If one node goes down, the rest of the network can still function.

Key Considerations for Node Communication

When designing the communication system for your blockchain network, there are several important factors to consider:

- Network Protocol: This defines the rules of engagement for how nodes interact. It specifies how nodes discover each other, establish connections, exchange information, and handle network disruptions.
- Message Format: Nodes need to speak the same language to understand each other. This involves defining a standard format for the messages exchanged between nodes, including things like message types, data structures, and encoding schemes.

- Security: Protecting the network from attacks and ensuring data integrity is paramount. This might involve using encryption to secure communication channels, implementing authentication mechanisms to verify node identities, and using digital signatures to prevent message tampering.
- Efficiency: The communication protocol should be optimized for speed and efficiency to minimize latency and bandwidth consumption. This is especially important for blockchains that need to handle a high volume of transactions.

Elixir's Networking Toolkit

Elixir provides a rich set of tools and libraries for building distributed applications and handling network communication. You can use these tools to implement your blockchain's network protocol and manage connections between nodes.

- TCP/IP Sockets: Elixir provides built-in support for TCP/IP sockets, which are the foundation of most internet communication. You can use sockets to establish connections between nodes and exchange data.
- GenTCP: This is an OTP behavior that provides a higher-level abstraction for working with TCP sockets. It simplifies the process of managing connections and handling incoming and outgoing data.
- Distributed Process Communication: Elixir allows you to spawn processes on different nodes and communicate between them using message passing.

This enables you to build truly distributed blockchain applications.

Example (Conceptual):

```elixir
# This is a simplified example, actual implementations are more complex

defmodule Node do
  use GenServer

  def start_link(name) do
    GenServer.start_link(__MODULE__, name, name: name)
  end

  def connect(node1, node2) do
    # Establish a TCP connection between the nodes
    {:ok, socket} = GenTCP.connect(node2.address, node2.port)

    # Send a connection message
    GenTCP.send(socket, "Hello from #{node1.name}")

    # Receive a response
    {:ok, response} = GenTCP.recv(socket, 0)

    IO.puts("Received: #{response}")
```

```
  end

  ## GenServer callbacks

  def init(name) do
    # ... initialize node state ...
  end

  def handle_info({:tcp, socket, data}, state) do
    # Handle incoming data from other nodes
    IO.puts("Received: #{data}")
    # Send a response
    GenTCP.send(socket, "Hello back from #{state.name}")
    {:noreply, state}
  end
end
```

This example demonstrates a simplified implementation of node communication using GenTCP. In a real-world scenario, you would need to implement more complex logic for node discovery, message handling, and error handling.

Real-World Examples

- Bitcoin: Uses a custom P2P network protocol that allows nodes to discover each other and exchange block and transaction data.

- Ethereum: Uses a protocol called "devp2p" for node discovery and communication.

Understanding the principles of node communication and leveraging Elixir's networking capabilities, you can design a robust and efficient communication system for your blockchain network.

5.4 Data Serialization and Storage

Computers think in terms of bits and bytes, while we humans think in terms of words, numbers, and structures. To bridge this gap, we need a way to translate our human-readable data into a format that computers can understand and store efficiently. This process is called serialization.

Think of it like translating a book from one language to another. You need to convert the words and sentences into the equivalent expressions in the target language while preserving the meaning of the text.

Why Serialize?

In blockchain, serialization is crucial for several reasons:

- Storage: Serialized data is typically more compact and efficient to store than its original form. This is important because blockchain data can grow very large over time.
- Transmission: Serialized data can be easily transmitted over a network. This is essential for nodes to communicate with each other and share information about transactions and blocks.

- Interoperability: Using a standard serialization format allows different systems and applications to interact with your blockchain.

Serialization Formats

There are several popular serialization formats used in blockchain and other applications:

- JSON (JavaScript Object Notation): This is a human-readable format that uses a simple text-based structure to represent data. It's widely used for data exchange on the web and is supported by many programming languages.
- Protocol Buffers: Developed by Google, Protocol Buffers is a binary serialization format that is more efficient and compact than JSON. It uses a schema definition language to define the structure of the data.
- MessagePack: This is another binary serialization format that is known for its compactness and efficiency. It's often used in applications where performance is critical.

Example: Serializing Data in Elixir

Elixir provides libraries for working with various serialization formats. Here's an example of how to serialize data using JSON:

```Elixir
iex> data = %{name: "Alice", age: 30}
%{age: 30, name: "Alice"}
```

```
iex> Poison.encode!(data)
```
"{\"age\":30,\"name\":\"Alice\"}"

This code snippet uses the Poison library to serialize a map into a JSON string.

Storing the Blockchain: Where Does the Data Go?

Once you've serialized your blockchain data, you need a place to store it. There are several options for storing blockchain data:

- LevelDB: This is a key-value store that is often used in blockchain implementations. It's efficient for storing and retrieving data based on keys.
- RocksDB: This is a more advanced key-value store that offers improved performance and features compared to LevelDB.
- IPFS (InterPlanetary File System): This is a decentralized storage system that can be used to store large files and data. It's often used in conjunction with blockchain to store large datasets or multimedia content.

The choice of storage solution depends on your blockchain's specific requirements. Consider factors like:

- Data Volume: How much data do you need to store?
- Performance: How fast do you need to access and retrieve data?
- Scalability: How will the storage solution handle the growing amount of data?

- Security: How will you protect the data from unauthorized access and tampering?

Elixir and Data Storage

Elixir provides libraries and tools for interacting with various data storage solutions. You can use these tools to store and retrieve your blockchain data efficiently.

Real-World Examples

- Bitcoin: Uses LevelDB to store the blockchain data.
- Ethereum: Uses a modified version of LevelDB.
- Filecoin: Uses IPFS to store files and data.

Understanding the concepts of data serialization and storage, and by leveraging Elixir's capabilities for data handling, you can design a robust and efficient system for managing your blockchain's valuable information.

Chapter 6: Implementing a Basic Blockchain in Elixir

Think of this chapter as a workshop where we'll craft our own mini-blockchain from scratch. We'll define the structure of blocks and transactions, implement a basic consensus mechanism, and even do some testing and debugging to ensure everything works smoothly.

6.1 Project: Building a Simple Blockchain

In this project, we're going to build a simple blockchain from the ground up using Elixir. This will give you a hands-on understanding of how the different pieces fit together and solidify the concepts we've covered so far.

Our Blockchain: A Digital Notebook

Think of our blockchain as a digital notebook where we can record entries, or "transactions," in a secure and tamper-proof way. Each page in this notebook represents a "block," and these blocks are chained together chronologically to form an immutable record of all entries.

Features of Our Simple Blockchain

Our blockchain will have the following features:

- Blocks: Each block will contain a timestamp, a list of transactions (which, for simplicity, will be text strings in this project), and the hash of the previous block.

- Chain: The blocks will be chained together, forming a chronological and tamper-proof record of transactions.
- Genesis Block: We'll start with a special block called the "genesis block," which is the first block in the chain.
- Proof-of-Work (PoW): We'll use a simplified version of the Proof-of-Work consensus mechanism to add new blocks to the chain. This involves finding a special number (called a nonce) that, when combined with the block data, produces a hash that meets certain criteria.
- Immutability: Once a block is added to the chain, it cannot be altered or removed.

Why Build a Simple Blockchain?

Building a simple blockchain might seem like a toy project, but it's incredibly valuable for learning the core concepts and mechanics of blockchain technology. By implementing the basic building blocks yourself, you'll gain a deeper understanding of how blockchains work under the hood.

This foundation will serve you well as you move on to more complex blockchain projects and explore advanced features like different consensus mechanisms, smart contracts, and decentralized applications.

Tools and Technologies

We'll be using the following tools and technologies for this project:

- Elixir: Our programming language of choice, known for its concurrency, fault-tolerance, and functional programming paradigm.
- Structs: Elixir's way of defining custom data structures to represent blocks and transactions.
- Cryptographic Hashing: We'll use Elixir's :crypto module to calculate hashes for our blocks.
- ExUnit: Elixir's built-in testing framework, which we'll use to write tests for our blockchain functions.

Project Structure

We'll organize our project into modules to keep our code clean and maintainable. We'll have modules for:

- Block: To define the structure of a block.
- Transaction: To define the structure of a transaction (although we'll keep it simple for now).
- Blockchain: To implement the core blockchain functionality, such as adding blocks, mining blocks, and validating the chain.

Getting Started

If you haven't already, make sure you have Elixir and Erlang installed on your system. You can then create a new Elixir project using the mix new command:

Bash

```
mix new simple_blockchain
```

This will create a new project directory with the necessary files. We can then start writing our code in the lib/simple_blockchain.ex file.

6.2 Creating Blocks and Transactions

We'll start by defining the fundamental building blocks: blocks and transactions. Think of these as the bricks and mortar of our blockchain structure.

Blocks

In our simple blockchain, each block will be like a container holding a set of transactions. It's like a page in our digital notebook, recording a snapshot of activity at a particular moment in time.

To represent a block in Elixir, we'll use a struct. Structs are a convenient way to group related data together and give it a meaningful structure.

Here's how we can define our Block struct:

Elixir

```elixir
defmodule Block do

  defstruct timestamp: nil, transactions: [], previous_hash: "", hash: ""

end
```

Let's break down what each field represents:

- timestamp: This field stores the timestamp of when the block was created. This helps us establish the order of blocks in the chain.
- transactions: This field stores a list of transactions included in the block. For our simple blockchain, these transactions will just be text strings.

- previous_hash: This field stores the hash of the previous block in the chain. This is crucial for linking the blocks together and ensuring immutability.
- hash: This field stores the hash of the current block. This hash is calculated based on the block's contents and serves as a unique fingerprint for the block.

Transactions

Transactions are the individual actions or data exchanges that are recorded on the blockchain. In a cryptocurrency blockchain, a transaction might represent a transfer of funds from one user to another. In a supply chain blockchain, it might represent the movement of goods from a warehouse to a store.

For our simple blockchain, we'll keep the transactions very basic. They will simply be text strings representing messages.

We can define a Transaction struct, even though it's not strictly necessary for our current project:

Elixir

```
defmodule Transaction do

  defstruct sender: "", receiver: "", amount: 0

end
```

This struct includes fields for sender, receiver, and amount, which would be relevant in a more complex blockchain. However, for now, we'll just be storing text strings directly in the transactions field of the Block struct.

Creating Blocks

To create a new block, we can use the %Block{} syntax and provide values for the fields:

```Elixir
# Create a new block with a timestamp and some transactions
block = %Block{
  timestamp: DateTime.utc_now(),
  transactions: ["Hello, blockchain!", "This is a test transaction."],
  previous_hash: "previous_block_hash",
  hash: "current_block_hash"
}
```

Of course, we'll need to calculate the actual hash of the block later, but this gives you an idea of how to create a Block struct.

Real-World Example: Bitcoin Blocks

In Bitcoin, blocks have a more complex structure than our simple example. They include fields like:

- Block version
- Previous block hash
- Merkle root (a hash that summarizes all transactions in the block)
- Timestamp

- Difficulty target (used for Proof-of-Work)
- Nonce (a random number used for Proof-of-Work)

By defining the structure of blocks and transactions, we've laid the groundwork for building our blockchain. In the next section, we'll explore how to implement a basic consensus mechanism to add new blocks to the chain.

6.3 Implementing a Basic Consensus Mechanism

Now that we have our blocks and transactions defined, let's talk about how we add new blocks to our blockchain. This is where consensus mechanisms come into play. They're the rules that ensure all nodes in the network agree on which blocks are valid and should be added to the chain.

For our simple blockchain, we'll implement a basic version of the Proof-of-Work (PoW) consensus mechanism. This is the same mechanism used by Bitcoin, although ours will be a simplified version to illustrate the core concepts.

Proof-of-Work: A Computational Challenge

In Proof-of-Work, adding a new block to the chain requires solving a computational puzzle. This puzzle involves finding a special number, called a nonce, that, when combined with the block data, produces a hash that meets certain criteria.

Think of it like a guessing game where you need to find a secret number that unlocks the block. This "guessing" involves a lot of computational work, making it difficult for anyone to manipulate the blockchain.

Our Simplified PoW

In our implementation, the criteria for a valid hash will be that it starts with a certain number of zeros. The more zeros required, the harder the puzzle is to solve. This number of zeros is called the "difficulty" of the puzzle.

Mining: The Search for the Nonce

The process of finding a valid nonce is called "mining." Miners (which in our case will just be our Elixir code) try different nonce values until they find one that produces a valid hash.

Implementing PoW in Elixir

Let's add the PoW logic to our Blockchain module:

```Elixir
defmodule Blockchain do

  defstruct chain: [], difficulty: 2

  def new() do

    %Blockchain{chain: [create_genesis_block()], difficulty: 2}

  end

  defp create_genesis_block() do

    %Block{timestamp: DateTime.utc_now(), transactions: [], previous_hash: "0"}

  end
```

```elixir
def add_block(blockchain, transactions) do
  previous_block = List.last(blockchain.chain)
  new_block = %Block{
    timestamp: DateTime.utc_now(),
    transactions: transactions,
    previous_hash: previous_block.hash
  }
  mined_block = mine_block(new_block, blockchain.difficulty)
  %Blockchain{blockchain | chain: blockchain.chain ++ [mined_block]}
end

defp mine_block(block, difficulty) do
  nonce = 0
  hash = calculate_hash(block, nonce)
  while String.slice(hash, 0, difficulty) != String.duplicate("0", difficulty) do
    nonce = nonce + 1
    hash = calculate_hash(block, nonce)
  end
  %Block{block | hash: hash, nonce: nonce}
end
```

```elixir
  defp calculate_hash(block, nonce) do
    block_string = "#{block.timestamp}#{block.transactions}#{block.previous_hash}#{nonce}"

    :crypto.hash(:sha256, block_string)
    |> Base.encode16(case: :lower)
  end
end
```

In this code:

- add_block creates a new block and then calls mine_block to find a valid nonce.
- mine_block iterates through nonce values until it finds one that produces a hash with the required number of leading zeros.
- calculate_hash calculates the hash of the block data combined with the nonce.

Real-World Example: Bitcoin Mining

In Bitcoin, mining is a competitive process where miners use specialized hardware to solve the PoW puzzle. The first miner to find a valid nonce broadcasts the block to the network, and if it's accepted, they receive a reward in Bitcoin.

In a real blockchain, the difficulty of the PoW puzzle is adjusted dynamically to ensure that blocks are added at a consistent rate. This prevents the blockchain from growing too quickly or too slowly.

In our simple blockchain, we'll keep the difficulty fixed for now. But you can experiment with adjusting the `difficulty` value in the `Blockchain` struct to see how it affects the time it takes to mine a block.

By implementing this basic PoW consensus mechanism, you've added a crucial piece to your blockchain puzzle. Now you have a way to add new blocks to the chain in a secure and verifiable way.

6.4 Testing and Debugging

We've built the core functionality of our blockchain, but how do we know it actually works correctly? That's where testing and debugging come in. Think of these as our quality assurance tools, ensuring that our code behaves as expected and catching any bugs or errors before they cause problems.

Testing: Ensuring Our Code Works

Testing is the process of verifying that our code functions correctly. We write tests that execute different parts of our code and check that the results match our expectations. This helps us catch errors early in the development process and ensures that our blockchain behaves reliably.

ExUnit: Elixir's Testing Framework

Elixir has a built-in testing framework called ExUnit. It provides a simple and convenient way to write and run tests.

Let's write a test case for our `Blockchain` module:

```elixir
defmodule BlockchainTest do
  use ExUnit.Case

  test "adding a new block" do
    # Create a new blockchain
    blockchain = Blockchain.new()

    # Add a block with some transactions
    new_blockchain = Blockchain.add_block(blockchain, ["Hello", "world!"])

    # Assert that the chain now has two blocks (genesis block + new block)
    assert length(new_blockchain.chain) == 2

    # Assert that the new block contains the correct transactions
    assert new_blockchain.chain |> List.last() |> Map.get(:transactions) == ["Hello", "world!"]
  end

  test "genesis block has previous hash of 0" do
    blockchain = Blockchain.new()
    genesis_block = List.first(blockchain.chain)
    assert genesis_block.previous_hash == "0"
  end
```

```
    # Add more test cases to cover other functions
and scenarios

end
```

In this test case, we:

1. Create a new blockchain using Blockchain.new().
2. Add a block with some transactions using Blockchain.add_block/2.
3. Assert that the chain now has two blocks (the genesis block and the new block).
4. Assert that the new block contains the correct transactions.

We can run our tests using the mix test command in the terminal. ExUnit will execute our test cases and report any failures.

Writing Effective Tests

Here are some tips for writing effective tests:

- Test individual units of code: Focus on testing small, isolated parts of your code (functions or modules) to pinpoint errors more easily.
- Cover different scenarios: Test your code with various inputs and edge cases to ensure it handles different situations correctly.
- Write clear and concise tests: Make your tests easy to read and understand so that you can quickly identify the source of any failures.

Debugging: Finding and Fixing Errors

Even with thorough testing, bugs can still slip through the cracks. Debugging is the process of identifying and fixing errors in your code.

Elixir provides several tools to help you debug your code:

- IO.inspect: This function allows you to print the value of a variable or expression to the console. This can be helpful for understanding the state of your program at different points.
- Debugger: Elixir has a built-in debugger that allows you to step through your code line by line, inspect variables, and set breakpoints.
- Logging: You can add logging statements to your code to track events and identify potential issues.

Real-World Example: Debugging a Smart Contract

Imagine you're developing a smart contract for a decentralized exchange. You deploy the contract to a test network, and you notice that users are able to withdraw more funds than they have deposited. This is a critical bug that needs to be fixed immediately.

You can use debugging tools to step through the contract's code, inspect the variables, and identify the logic error that is causing this vulnerability. Once you've found the bug, you can fix it and redeploy the contract.

Testing and debugging are essential skills for any blockchain developer. By mastering these skills, you can ensure that your blockchain applications are robust, reliable, and secure.

Chapter 7: Advanced Blockchain Features

Now that we've built a basic blockchain, let's explore some advanced features that can make our blockchain more powerful, efficient, and versatile. Think of this as adding some cool gadgets and upgrades to our blockchain toolbox.

7.1 State Channels and Off-Chain Transactions

Let's discuss a clever technique that can significantly boost the scalability and efficiency of blockchain applications: state channels. As you know, blockchains can sometimes get a bit congested when there's a high volume of transactions. State channels offer a way to alleviate this congestion by moving some of those transactions off the main blockchain.

Think of it like this:

You and your friend love playing online games together, and you often bet small amounts of cryptocurrency on the outcome. Instead of recording each tiny bet on the main blockchain, which can be slow and expensive, you could open a "state channel" – a private channel just between the two of you.

You can then make as many bets as you want off-chain, updating the balance between yourselves without involving the main blockchain. When you're done playing for the day, you close the channel and settle the final balance on the main blockchain. This way, only the final result needs to be recorded on the blockchain, saving time and resources.

How State Channels Work

1. Opening the Channel: To open a state channel, participants deposit some funds into a multi-signature wallet. This wallet requires the signatures of both participants to release the funds.
2. Transacting Off-Chain: Participants can then make as many transactions as they want off-chain. These transactions are signed by both parties and update the balance between them.
3. Closing the Channel: When the participants are finished transacting, they close the channel. The final state of the channel, including the final balance, is recorded on the main blockchain.

Benefits of State Channels:

- Scalability: State channels allow you to handle a large number of transactions without clogging up the main blockchain. This is because only the final settlement needs to be recorded on the chain.
- Speed: Transactions within a state channel are instant, as you don't have to wait for block confirmations on the main blockchain.
- Privacy: Transactions within a state channel are only visible to the participants involved. This provides an extra layer of privacy compared to transactions on the public blockchain.

- Reduced Costs: By minimizing the number of on-chain transactions, state channels can significantly reduce transaction fees.

Real-World Example: Lightning Network

The Lightning Network is a popular example of state channels implemented on the Bitcoin blockchain. It enables fast and cheap Bitcoin transactions by allowing users to create payment channels between each other.

Elixir and State Channels

Elixir's concurrency and fault-tolerance features make it a great choice for building state channel infrastructure. You can use Elixir processes to manage channels, handle off-chain transactions, and ensure secure communication between participants.

Example (Conceptual):

```elixir
# This is a simplified example, actual implementations are more complex

defmodule StateChannel do

  def open_channel(participant1, participant2, initial_balance) do

    # Create a multi-signature wallet

    wallet = MultiSigWallet.new(participant1, participant2)

    # Deposit initial funds into the wallet
```

```elixir
    wallet.deposit(participant1, initial_balance)

    # Create a state channel process
    {:ok, pid} = StateChannelProcess.start_link(wallet, initial_balance)

    pid
  end

  def close_channel(pid) do
    # Send a message to the state channel process to close the channel
    send(pid, :close)
  end
end

defmodule StateChannelProcess do
  use GenServer

  def start_link(wallet, initial_balance) do
    GenServer.start_link(__MODULE__, {wallet, initial_balance}, name: __MODULE__)
  end

  # ... handle off-chain transactions and channel closure ...
end
```

This example demonstrates a simplified implementation of opening and closing a state channel. In a real-world scenario, you would need to implement more complex logic for handling transactions, managing channel state, and ensuring security.

By understanding the concept of state channels and leveraging Elixir's capabilities, you can build blockchain applications that are more scalable, efficient, and private.

7.2 Cross-Chain Interoperability

Alright, let's talk about connecting different blockchains! You see, the blockchain space is a bit like a world with different countries, each with its own currency, rules, and culture. Cross-chain interoperability is like building bridges between these countries, allowing them to interact and exchange value.

Think of it this way: wouldn't it be cool if you could easily use your Bitcoin to buy something on the Ethereum network, or transfer data from a Hyperledger Fabric blockchain to a Corda blockchain? That's the goal of cross-chain interoperability.

Why is Cross-Chain Interoperability Important?

- Increased Functionality: Different blockchains have different strengths and weaknesses. By connecting them, you can leverage the best features of each chain. For example, you might use Bitcoin for its security and stability, while using Ethereum for its smart contract capabilities.

- Enhanced Liquidity: Cross-chain interoperability allows assets to flow freely between different blockchains, increasing liquidity and market efficiency.
- Collaboration and Innovation: It enables different blockchain projects to collaborate and build on each other's work, fostering innovation and accelerating the development of new applications.
- Unified Ecosystem: Ultimately, cross-chain interoperability can lead to a more unified and interconnected blockchain ecosystem, where different chains work together seamlessly.

Approaches to Cross-Chain Interoperability

There are several approaches to achieving cross-chain interoperability, each with its own trade-offs:

1. Atomic Swaps

Atomic swaps allow you to exchange cryptocurrencies directly between different blockchains without the need for a trusted intermediary. It's like a simultaneous swap of goods between two parties, where either both parties get what they agreed on, or the transaction is canceled entirely.

This is achieved through the use of smart contracts that lock up the funds on both chains until both parties fulfill their part of the agreement.

2. Sidechains

A sidechain is a separate blockchain that is interoperable with a main blockchain. It's like a smaller, specialized country that has a close relationship with a larger country.

Sidechains can be used to experiment with new features or implement specific use cases without affecting the main chain. They can also be used to transfer assets between different blockchains.

3. Relays

A relay is an intermediate blockchain that acts as a bridge between two or more other blockchains. It's like a central hub that connects different countries.

Relays can facilitate communication and asset transfer between different blockchains, even if those blockchains are not directly compatible.

Real-World Examples

- Polkadot: A blockchain platform that focuses on cross-chain interoperability. It allows different blockchains to connect and communicate with each other through a central "relay chain."
- Cosmos: Another platform that aims to create an "internet of blockchains." It uses a technology called "IBC" (Inter-Blockchain Communication) to enable interoperability between different chains.
- Wanchain: A blockchain platform that focuses on decentralized cross-chain transactions. It allows

users to transfer assets between different blockchains without relying on centralized exchanges.

Elixir and Cross-Chain Interoperability

Elixir can be used to build bridges and interoperability solutions between different blockchains. You can use Elixir to:

- Implement communication protocols: Develop the communication protocols that allow different blockchains to exchange information and transfer assets.
- Handle data translation: Translate data between different blockchain formats and data structures.
- Manage asset transfers: Implement the logic for securely transferring assets between different chains.

Example (Conceptual):

```elixir
# This is a simplified example, actual
implementations are more complex

defmodule CrossChainBridge do

  def transfer(source_chain, destination_chain, asset, amount) do

    # Lock the asset on the source chain

    source_chain.lock_asset(asset, amount)

    # Generate a proof of the lock

    proof = source_chain.generate_proof()
```

```
    # Send the proof and transfer request to the destination chain
    destination_chain.verify_proof(proof)
    destination_chain.unlock_asset(asset, amount)
  end
end
```

This example demonstrates a simplified implementation of a cross-chain bridge. In a real-world scenario, you would need to implement more complex logic for handling different blockchain protocols, security considerations, and error handling.

By understanding the concepts of cross-chain interoperability and leveraging Elixir's capabilities, you can contribute to building a more interconnected and functional blockchain ecosystem.

7.3 Privacy-Enhancing Techniques

While transparency is often touted as a key feature of blockchain, there are situations where you might want to keep certain information confidential. That's where privacy-enhancing techniques come in.

Think of it like this: you might want to share your financial transactions with your accountant, but you probably don't want your nosy neighbor to see them. Similarly, in blockchain, there are times when you need to protect sensitive data while still maintaining the integrity and transparency of the system.

Why is Privacy Important in Blockchain?

- Protecting Sensitive Information: Some blockchain applications deal with sensitive data, such as financial transactions, medical records, or personal identities. Privacy-enhancing techniques help protect this information from prying eyes.
- Compliance with Regulations: Many industries have regulations that require the protection of sensitive data. Privacy-enhancing techniques can help blockchain applications comply with these regulations.
- Commercial Sensitivity: Businesses might want to keep certain information, such as trade secrets or financial strategies, confidential from competitors.
- Fungibility: In the context of cryptocurrencies, fungibility means that all units of the currency are interchangeable. Privacy-enhancing techniques can help ensure fungibility by preventing the tracking and tracing of specific coins.

Techniques for Enhancing Privacy

Let's explore some of the most common privacy-enhancing techniques used in blockchain:

1. Zero-Knowledge Proofs (ZKPs)

ZKPs are a cryptographic marvel that allows one party (the prover) to prove to another party (the verifier) that they know a certain piece of information without revealing the information itself.

It's like proving you know the solution to a Sudoku puzzle without showing the actual solution. You can convince someone that you've solved it by revealing only a few selected numbers, enough to demonstrate your knowledge without giving away the entire solution.

ZKPs can be used in blockchain to:

- Verify identity without revealing personal details.
- Prove ownership of an asset without disclosing the asset itself.
- Conduct private transactions without revealing the transaction amounts.

2. Confidential Transactions

Confidential transactions use cryptography to encrypt transaction details, such as the sender, receiver, and amount, while still allowing the network to verify the validity of the transaction.

It's like sending a sealed envelope with a message inside. The recipient can verify that the envelope is authentic and hasn't been tampered with, but they can't see the message inside until they open it.

3. Ring Signatures

Ring signatures allow a user to sign a transaction on behalf of a group of users, without revealing their individual identity.

It's like signing a petition with a group of people. The petition shows that a certain number of people signed it, but it doesn't reveal who signed it specifically.

Real-World Examples

- Zcash: A privacy-focused cryptocurrency that uses zero-knowledge proofs to shield transaction details.
- Monero: Another privacy-focused cryptocurrency that uses ring signatures and confidential transactions.
- Aztec Network: A privacy layer for Ethereum that uses ZKPs to enable private transactions and smart contracts.

Elixir and Privacy-Enhancing Techniques

While Elixir doesn't have built-in support for all of these techniques, you can use it to integrate with libraries and tools that provide this functionality. For example, you could use Elixir to:

- Integrate with ZKP libraries: Use libraries like snarky or zexe to implement ZKPs in your Elixir applications.
- Build confidential transaction schemes: Use Elixir's cryptographic libraries to implement confidential transaction schemes.
- Develop privacy-focused blockchain applications: Create blockchain applications that prioritize privacy using these techniques.

Example (Conceptual):

```elixir
# This is a simplified example, actual implementations are more complex

defmodule PrivateTransaction do
```

```
    def send(sender, receiver, amount) do

    # Encrypt the transaction details

    encrypted_data = encrypt(sender, receiver, amount)

    # Create a zero-knowledge proof that the transaction is valid

    proof = generate_proof(encrypted_data)

    # Send the encrypted data and proof to the blockchain

    Blockchain.add_transaction(encrypted_data, proof)

  end
end
```

This example demonstrates a simplified implementation of a private transaction using encryption and zero-knowledge proofs. In a real-world scenario, you would need to implement more complex logic for key management, proof generation, and verification.

7.4 Decentralized Storage (IPFS)

Blockchains are great for storing transaction history and small pieces of information, but they're not always the best choice for storing large files or datasets. That's where decentralized storage solutions like IPFS (InterPlanetary File System) come in.

Think of it like this: you wouldn't store your entire photo library directly in your email inbox, would you? It would quickly become cluttered and inefficient. Instead, you might use a cloud storage service like Dropbox or Google Drive to store your photos and then share links to them in your emails.

Similarly, IPFS provides a decentralized way to store and share files, complementing the capabilities of blockchain technology.

IPFS is a peer-to-peer (P2P) network for storing and sharing files. It's like a giant, distributed hard drive that anyone can contribute to. Instead of relying on centralized servers, IPFS distributes files across a network of computers, making it more resilient to censorship and single points of failure.

Content Addressing

One of the key innovations of IPFS is content addressing. In traditional file systems, files are identified by their location (e.g., C:\Users\Documents\my_file.txt). In IPFS, files are identified by their content.

When you add a file to IPFS, it's given a unique content identifier (CID), which is essentially a hash of the file's contents. This means that the same file will always have the same CID, regardless of where it's stored on the network.

Benefits of IPFS

- Efficiency: By distributing data across the network, IPFS reduces storage costs and improves efficiency.

- Resilience: IPFS makes data more resilient to censorship and single points of failure. If one node goes down, other nodes can still provide access to the data.
- Immutability: Once a file is added to IPFS, it cannot be tampered with. This ensures data integrity and prevents unauthorized modifications.
- Deduplication: IPFS automatically deduplicates files, meaning it only stores one copy of a file, even if it's added multiple times. This saves storage space and bandwidth.

Real-World Examples

- Filecoin: A decentralized storage network that uses IPFS to store data. Users can pay to store their data on the network, and miners earn rewards for providing storage space.
- NFT Storage: A service that uses IPFS and Filecoin to store NFT data, making NFTs more resilient and persistent.
- DWeb (Decentralized Web): IPFS is a key building block for the DWeb, a vision of a more decentralized and user-centric internet.

Elixir and IPFS

Elixir can be used to build applications that interact with IPFS. There are Elixir libraries that provide APIs for:

- Adding and retrieving files: Upload and download files to and from the IPFS network.
- Managing data storage: Pin files to your local node to ensure they remain available.

- Integrating IPFS with blockchain: Store large datasets or multimedia content on IPFS and link them to your blockchain application.

Example (Conceptual):

```elixir
# This is a simplified example, actual implementations are more complex

defmodule IPFSHelper do

  def upload_file(file_path) do
    # Use an IPFS client library to upload the file
    {:ok, cid} = IPFS.Client.add(file_path)
    cid
  end

  def download_file(cid, output_path) do
    # Use an IPFS client library to download the file
    IPFS.Client.get(cid, output_path)
  end

end
```

This example demonstrates a simplified implementation of uploading and downloading files using an IPFS client library. In a real-world scenario, you would need to handle error conditions, manage connections to the IPFS network, and potentially pin files for persistence.

Understanding the capabilities of IPFS and leveraging Elixir's strengths, you can build decentralized applications that efficiently store and manage large amounts of data.

Chapter 8: Building Decentralized Applications (DApps)

It's time to take everything we've learned about blockchain and Elixir and put it together to build something truly amazing: decentralized applications, or DApps! These are applications that run on a blockchain network, offering users greater security, transparency, and control over their data.

Think of DApps as the next generation of web applications. Instead of relying on centralized servers and intermediaries, they leverage the power of blockchain to create a more open, democratic, and user-centric internet.

8.1 Introduction to DApps

DApps, or decentralized applications are a new breed of applications that leverage the unique properties of blockchain technology to offer users greater security, transparency, and control.

Think of DApps as the evolution of web applications. Traditional web apps rely on centralized servers and intermediaries, which can be vulnerable to censorship, hacking, and downtime. DApps, on the other hand, distribute their backend logic and data across a decentralized network, making them more resilient and resistant to these issues.

Key Characteristics of DApps

Let's break down what makes DApps so special:

- Decentralized Backend: Instead of relying on a central server, DApps run on a decentralized blockchain network. This means there's no single point of failure or control. If one node in the network goes down, the application can still function. This also makes them resistant to censorship, as no single entity can shut down the application.
- Open Source: The code for many DApps is open source, meaning anyone can inspect, audit, and contribute to it. This promotes transparency and allows the community to participate in the development and improvement of the application.
- Cryptographic Security: DApps use cryptography to secure data and ensure the integrity of transactions. This makes them highly resistant to hacking and fraud. User data is protected by cryptographic keys, and transactions are verified and validated by the network.
- Tokenization: Many DApps use tokens to incentivize user participation and govern the application's operation. These tokens can represent voting rights, access to premium features, or even ownership in the application itself. This creates a more democratic and community-driven approach to application development.

Examples of DApps in Action

To give you a better idea of what DApps can do, let's look at some real-world examples:

- Cryptocurrency Wallets: MetaMask and Trust Wallet are examples of DApps that allow users to securely store and manage their cryptocurrencies. They provide a user-friendly interface for interacting with the blockchain and conducting transactions.
- Decentralized Exchanges (DEXs): Uniswap and SushiSwap are examples of DEXs that allow users to trade cryptocurrencies directly with each other without relying on centralized exchanges. These DEXs use smart contracts to automate the trading process and ensure security.
- NFT Marketplaces: OpenSea and Rarible are examples of NFT marketplaces where users can buy, sell, and trade non-fungible tokens (NFTs). These marketplaces use blockchain to track ownership and ensure the authenticity of NFTs.
- Decentralized Social Media: Mastodon and Minds are examples of decentralized social media platforms that aim to give users more control over their data and reduce censorship. They use blockchain to distribute content and manage user accounts.
- Prediction Markets: Augur and Gnosis are examples of prediction markets where users can bet on the outcome of future events. These platforms use blockchain to track bets and ensure fair payouts.

Benefits of DApps

DApps offer several advantages over traditional web applications:

- Censorship Resistance: No single entity can control or censor the application, as it runs on a decentralized network.
- Security: Data is protected by cryptography and distributed across the network, making it more difficult to hack or compromise.
- Transparency: The code and operation of the application are open and transparent, allowing users to understand how it works and verify its integrity.
- Immutability: Data stored on the blockchain is tamper-proof and permanent, ensuring a reliable and auditable record of activity.

Challenges of DApps

While DApps offer many benefits, they also face some challenges:

- Scalability: Blockchain networks can be slower and less scalable than centralized servers, which can affect the performance of DApps.
- Usability: DApps can sometimes be more complex to use than traditional web applications, as they require users to interact with blockchain concepts like wallets and private keys.
- Development Complexity: Building DApps can be more complex than building traditional web applications, as it requires knowledge of blockchain technology and smart contract development.

Despite these challenges, DApps have the potential to revolutionize the way we build and use applications. As blockchain technology continues to evolve and mature, we can expect to see more innovative and impactful DApps emerge, offering users greater control, security, and transparency in their online interactions.

8.2 Connecting Elixir Blockchain to Front-End Interfaces

We've built the backend logic and data storage, but now we need a way for users to access and interact with our decentralized application (DApp). This is where front-end interfaces come in.

Think of the front-end as the face of your DApp. It's what users see and interact with — the buttons, forms, and displays that allow them to access the functionality of your blockchain.

Choosing Your Front-End Technology

You have a wide range of options when it comes to choosing a front-end technology for your DApp. Some popular choices include:

- React: A JavaScript library that's widely used for building user interfaces. It's known for its component-based architecture and flexibility.
- Vue.js: Another popular JavaScript framework that's easy to learn and use. It's known for its simplicity and performance.

- Angular: A comprehensive framework for building complex web applications. It's known for its structure and scalability.

The best choice for your DApp will depend on your specific needs and preferences. Consider factors like the complexity of your application, your team's experience, and the available libraries and tools for each framework.

Building a Bridge: The API

To connect your front-end to your Elixir blockchain, you'll need to create an API (Application Programming Interface). This API acts as a bridge, allowing your front-end to send requests to your blockchain and receive responses.

You can build your API using Elixir's Phoenix framework, which is a powerful web framework that's well-suited for building APIs. Phoenix provides features like routing, request handling, and JSON encoding, making it easy to create a robust and efficient API.

Example using Phoenix:

```elixir
# In your router.ex file

scope "/api", MyAppWeb do
  pipe_through :api

  get "/blocks/:block_number", BlockchainController, :get_block

  post "/transactions", BlockchainController, :send_transaction
```

```elixir
end

# In your blockchain_controller.ex file

defmodule MyAppWeb.BlockchainController do
  use MyAppWeb, :controller

  alias MyApp.Blockchain

  def get_block(conn, %{"block_number" => block_number}) do
    block = Blockchain.get_block(String.to_integer(block_number))
    json(conn, block)
  end

  def send_transaction(conn, %{"sender" => sender, "receiver" => receiver, "amount" => amount}) do
    with {:ok, transaction} <- Blockchain.send_transaction(sender, receiver, String.to_integer(amount)) do
      json(conn, transaction)
    end
  end
end
```

This example demonstrates a simple API with two endpoints:

- **/api/blocks/:block_number**: Retrieves a block by its number.
- **/api/transactions**: Sends a new transaction to the blockchain.

JavaScript Libraries

On the front-end side, you'll need a JavaScript library to interact with your blockchain's API. Some popular libraries include:

- Web3.js: A library for interacting with Ethereum and other EVM-compatible blockchains.
- Ethers.js: Another library for interacting with Ethereum, known for its simplicity and security.

These libraries provide functions for:

- Connecting to the blockchain: Establish a connection to your blockchain network.
- Sending transactions: Create and send transactions to the blockchain.
- Reading data: Retrieve data from the blockchain, such as account balances, transaction history, and smart contract state.
- Interacting with smart contracts: Call functions and read data from smart contracts deployed on the blockchain.

Example using Web3.js:

```javascript
// Replace with your API endpoint
const web3 = new Web3("http://localhost:4000");
```

```
async function getBlock(blockNumber) {

  const block = await web3.eth.getBlock(blockNumber);

  console.log(block);

}

async function sendTransaction(sender, receiver, amount) {

  const transaction = await web3.eth.sendTransaction({

    from: sender,

    to: receiver,

    value: amount

  });

  console.log(transaction);

}
```

This example demonstrates how to use Web3.js to interact with the API endpoints we defined earlier.

Real-World Example: MetaMask

MetaMask is a popular browser extension that acts as a cryptocurrency wallet and gateway to DApps. It provides a user-friendly interface for managing accounts, sending transactions, and interacting with DApps. MetaMask uses a combination of front-end technologies and JavaScript libraries to connect to different blockchain networks and DApps.

8.3 Example DApp Implementations

We've covered the fundamentals of DApps and how to connect our Elixir blockchain to a front-end interface. Now, let's explore some concrete examples of DApps that you can build to solidify your understanding and spark your creativity.

1. Decentralized To-Do List

This is a classic DApp example that demonstrates the basic principles of blockchain interaction. Instead of storing your to-do list on a centralized server, we'll store it on our Elixir blockchain, ensuring that your tasks are tamper-proof and persistent.

Features:

- Add Tasks: Users can add new tasks to their list.
- Mark as Complete: Users can mark tasks as complete.
- Remove Tasks: Users can remove tasks from their list.
- View Tasks: Users can view their list of tasks, including their status (complete or incomplete).

Implementation:

- Blockchain Logic: Use your Elixir blockchain to store the tasks. Each task can be represented as a transaction with fields like `task_id`, `description`, and `status`.
- API: Create an API with endpoints for adding, updating, and retrieving tasks.

- Front-End: Build a user interface with forms for adding tasks and buttons for marking them as complete or removing them.

Example Code Snippet (Elixir API):

```elixir
defmodule MyAppWeb.TaskController do
  use MyAppWeb, :controller
  alias MyApp.Blockchain

  def add_task(conn, %{"description" => description}) do
    with {:ok, task} <- Blockchain.add_task(description) do
      json(conn, task)
    end
  end

  def update_task(conn, %{"task_id" => task_id, "status" => status}) do
    with {:ok, task} <- Blockchain.update_task(task_id, status) do
      json(conn, task)
    end
  end
end
```

2. Decentralized Voting System

This DApp allows users to vote on proposals in a secure and transparent manner. The blockchain ensures that votes are tamper-proof and auditable.

Features:

- Create Proposals: Users can create new proposals for voting.
- Cast Votes: Users can cast their votes on proposals.
- View Results: Users can view the results of the voting.

Implementation:

- Blockchain Logic: Store proposals and votes on your Elixir blockchain. Each proposal can have fields like proposal_id, description, and options. Votes can be recorded as transactions associated with a proposal.
- API: Create an API with endpoints for creating proposals, casting votes, and retrieving results.
- Front-End: Build a user interface that displays proposals and allows users to cast their votes.

Example Code Snippet (Elixir API):

```elixir
defmodule MyAppWeb.VoteController do
  use MyAppWeb, :controller

  alias MyApp.Blockchain

  def cast_vote(conn, %{"proposal_id" => proposal_id, "vote" => vote}) do
```

```
    with {:ok, vote_record} <-
Blockchain.cast_vote(proposal_id, vote) do
      json(conn, vote_record)
    end
  end
end
```

3. Decentralized File Storage

This DApp allows users to store and share files on IPFS, a decentralized storage network. The blockchain is used to track ownership and ensure the integrity of the files.

Features:

- Upload Files: Users can upload files to IPFS.
- Share Files: Users can share files with others by providing the file's CID (content identifier).
- Verify Integrity: Users can verify the integrity of a file by comparing its hash with the hash stored on the blockchain.

Implementation:

- Blockchain Logic: Store the CID (content identifier) of each uploaded file on your Elixir blockchain, along with information about the file's owner and permissions.
- API: Create an API with endpoints for uploading files, retrieving file information, and managing access control.

- Front-End: Build a user interface that allows users to upload and share files.

Example Code Snippet (Elixir API):

```elixir
defmodule MyAppWeb.FileController do
  use MyAppWeb, :controller

  alias MyApp.Blockchain
  alias MyApp.IPFSHelper

  def upload_file(conn, %{"file" => file}) do
    # Upload the file to IPFS
    cid = IPFSHelper.upload_file(file.path)
    # Store the CID on the blockchain
    with {:ok, file_record} <- Blockchain.add_file(cid, file.filename) do
      json(conn, file_record)
    end
  end
end
```

Real-World Examples

- OpenBazaar: A decentralized marketplace that allows users to buy and sell goods and services directly with each other.

- Augur: A decentralized prediction market that allows users to bet on the outcome of future events.
- Aragon: A platform for creating and managing decentralized organizations.

Implementations of these examples of DApp and experimenting with your own ideas, can unlock the full potential of Elixir and blockchain to build innovative and impactful decentralized applications.

Chapter 9: Deploying and Scaling Your Blockchain

This chapter is all about taking your blockchain from a local project to a live, functioning network that can handle real-world demands. We'll explore deployment strategies, cloud platforms, containerization, performance optimization, and the ongoing care and feeding of your blockchain.

9.1 Deployment Strategies

Deploying a blockchain application is like setting up a network of interconnected spaceships. Each spaceship (or node) needs to be configured correctly, communicate effectively with others, and be ready to handle the demands of space travel (or in our case, processing transactions and securing the blockchain).

Factors to Consider When Choosing a Deployment Strategy

Before we explore the different deployment options, let's consider some key factors that will influence your decision:

- Network Type: What type of blockchain are you deploying? Is it a public, permissionless blockchain like Bitcoin, where anyone can join the network? Or is it a private, permissioned blockchain, where access is restricted to authorized participants? This will significantly impact your infrastructure choices and security considerations.

- Security: Security is paramount in the blockchain world.[1] You need to protect your nodes from attacks, secure your network communication, and ensure the integrity of your data.[2] This might involve using firewalls, intrusion detection systems, and secure key management practices.
- Scalability: How many users and transactions do you expect your blockchain to handle? Your deployment strategy should be able to scale to meet future demand. This might involve using cloud services, load balancing, and distributed storage solutions.
- Performance: How important is speed and efficiency? You'll want to optimize your deployment for performance to provide a smooth user experience. This might involve using high-performance servers, optimizing your code, and choosing efficient data structures.
- Cost: Consider the costs of different deployment options, including server costs, bandwidth, and maintenance. Balancing cost-effectiveness with performance and security is essential.

Deployment Options: Finding the Right Launchpad

Now, let's explore some common deployment options:

- Bare Metal: This involves deploying your blockchain directly on physical servers that you own or lease.[3] This gives you maximum control over your infrastructure but also requires more management and maintenance. You're responsible for setting up the servers, installing the operating system, configuring the network, and ensuring security.

- Virtual Machines (VMs): VMs are like software emulations of physical servers.[4] They provide a more flexible and scalable option than bare metal. You can easily provision and manage VMs in the cloud, scaling your resources up or down as needed.[5] Cloud providers like AWS, Azure, and Google Cloud offer a wide range of VM options.[6]
- Containers: Containers are a lightweight and portable way to package and deploy your blockchain application.[7] They bundle your application code and its dependencies into a self-contained unit that can be run on any system with a container runtime (like Docker) installed.[8] This makes it easy to deploy your blockchain on different platforms and environments.
- Serverless: Serverless platforms, like AWS Lambda or Google Cloud Functions, allow you to deploy your code without managing servers.[9] You simply upload your code, and the platform takes care of the underlying infrastructure. This can be a cost-effective and scalable option for certain types of blockchain applications.

Real-World Examples

- Bitcoin: Bitcoin is primarily deployed on bare metal servers run by miners around the world. This decentralized approach contributes to its security and censorship resistance.
- Ethereum: Ethereum nodes can be deployed on various platforms, including bare metal, VMs, and cloud services.

- Hyperledger Fabric: Hyperledger Fabric, an enterprise blockchain platform, is often deployed using containers and cloud services for flexibility and scalability.

The best deployment strategy for your blockchain depends on your specific needs and priorities. Consider the factors we discussed earlier, such as network type, security, scalability, performance, and cost, to make an informed decision.

9.2 Cloud Platforms and Containerization

Cloud platforms are like giant data centers that provide a wide range of services for running applications, including blockchain networks. They offer the infrastructure, tools, and flexibility to make deploying and scaling your blockchain a smoother process.

Why the Cloud?

Cloud platforms offer several advantages for blockchain deployment:

- Scalability: Easily scale your resources up or down as needed to handle fluctuations in demand.
- Flexibility: Choose from a variety of services and configurations to meet your specific needs.
- Cost-Effectiveness: Pay only for the resources you use, avoiding the upfront costs of hardware and infrastructure.
- Reliability: Cloud providers offer high availability and redundancy to ensure your blockchain runs smoothly.

- Security: Cloud platforms provide security features like firewalls, intrusion detection systems, and encryption to protect your blockchain.

Popular Cloud Platforms

Some of the most popular cloud platforms for blockchain deployment include:

- Amazon Web Services (AWS): AWS offers a comprehensive suite of services, including virtual machines (EC2), storage (S3), databases (RDS), and blockchain-specific services like Amazon Managed Blockchain.
- Microsoft Azure: Azure provides similar services to AWS, including virtual machines, storage, databases, and blockchain services like Azure Blockchain Service.
- Google Cloud Platform (GCP): GCP offers a range of services, including virtual machines (Compute Engine), storage (Cloud Storage), databases (Cloud SQL), and blockchain services like Google Cloud Blockchain Platform.

Choosing a Cloud Platform

The best cloud platform for your blockchain will depend on your specific needs and preferences. Consider factors like:

- Services Offered: Does the platform offer the specific services you need, such as virtual machines, databases, and blockchain-specific tools?
- Pricing: Compare the pricing models of different platforms to find the most cost-effective option.

- Regions and Availability Zones: Choose a platform with regions and availability zones that are close to your users to minimize latency.
- Support and Documentation: Look for a platform with good documentation and support resources.

Containerization: Packaging Your Blockchain

Containerization is a powerful technique for packaging and deploying applications, including blockchain networks. It involves bundling your application code and its dependencies into a self-contained unit called a container. This container can then be run on any system that has a container runtime (like Docker) installed.

Benefits of Containerization

- Portability: Deploy your blockchain on different cloud platforms, on-premises servers, or even your local machine without compatibility issues.
- Consistency: Ensures your application runs the same way in different environments, reducing the risk of unexpected behavior.
- Isolation: Isolates your application from other applications and the host system, improving security and stability.
- Efficiency: Containers are generally more lightweight and efficient than virtual machines, reducing resource usage.

Docker: The Containerization King

Docker is the most popular containerization technology. It provides tools for building, sharing, and running containers.

Dockerfile Example:

```
Dockerfile

FROM elixir:1.14  # Use the official Elixir image as the base

WORKDIR /app  # Set the working directory inside the container

COPY mix.exs mix.lock ./  # Copy your project files

RUN mix deps.get  # Install dependencies

COPY . .  # Copy the rest of your application code

CMD ["mix", "phx.server"]  # Command to run your application
```

This Dockerfile defines the steps to build a Docker image for your Elixir blockchain application. You can then use this image to create and run containers on any system with Docker installed.

Orchestrating Containers with Kubernetes

For more complex deployments, you can use Kubernetes, a container orchestration platform. Kubernetes automates the deployment, scaling, and management of containers, making it easier to run your blockchain network across multiple servers.

Real-World Examples

- **Hyperledger Fabric:** Hyperledger Fabric, an enterprise blockchain platform, often uses Docker containers for deployment and Kubernetes for orchestration.
- **Quorum:** An enterprise-focused version of Ethereum, also utilizes Docker and Kubernetes for deployment and management.

Combining the power of cloud platforms and containerization, you can create a flexible, scalable, and cost-effective deployment strategy for your Elixir blockchain.

9.3 Performance Optimization and Scaling

Let's talk about making your blockchain fast and efficient! Just like a finely tuned race car, your blockchain needs to be optimized for performance to handle a high volume of transactions and users without slowing down. And as your blockchain grows, you'll need to scale it to meet increasing demand.

Performance Optimization

Think of performance optimization as fine-tuning the engine of your blockchain. You want to make sure every component is running smoothly and efficiently.

Here are some key areas to focus on:

- Code Optimization: Start with the foundation – your Elixir code. Use profiling tools to identify bottlenecks and optimize your code for speed and efficiency. This might involve using efficient algorithms, minimizing

memory allocations, and avoiding unnecessary computations.
- Database Optimization: Your blockchain likely uses a database to store data. Choose a database that's well-suited for your needs and optimize its configuration for performance. This might involve indexing key fields, optimizing queries, and using caching mechanisms.
- Network Optimization: Efficient network communication is crucial for a distributed system like a blockchain. Minimize latency and bandwidth usage by optimizing your network protocols and configurations. This might involve using efficient message formats, compressing data, and optimizing network topology.
- Caching: Caching involves storing frequently accessed data in a fast-access location, like memory. This can significantly reduce the load on your blockchain nodes and improve response times. You can use Elixir's built-in caching mechanisms or leverage external caching systems like Redis.

Example: Code Optimization

Elixir

```elixir
# Inefficient code
def process_transactions(transactions) do
  Enum.map(transactions, fn transaction ->
    # ... perform expensive operation on transaction ...
  end)
```

```
end

# Optimized code using Enum.reduce
def process_transactions(transactions) do
  Enum.reduce(transactions, [], fn transaction, acc ->
    # ... perform expensive operation on transaction ...
    [result | acc]
  end)
  |> Enum.reverse()
end
```

In this example, the optimized code uses Enum.reduce instead of Enum.map to avoid creating intermediate lists, which can improve performance for large lists of transactions.

Scaling

Scaling your blockchain is like expanding your racetrack to accommodate more cars. You need to make sure your infrastructure can handle the increased traffic and demand.

Here are some scaling techniques:

- Vertical Scaling: This involves increasing the resources of your existing nodes, such as adding more CPU, memory, or storage. This can be a quick and easy way to scale, but it has limitations, as you can only add so much to a single machine.
- Horizontal Scaling: This involves adding more nodes to your network to distribute the load. This is a more

scalable approach, as you can add as many nodes as needed. However, it requires careful management of network communication and data synchronization.
- Sharding: Sharding involves dividing your blockchain into smaller "shards," each handling a portion of the network's transactions and data. This can significantly improve scalability, as each shard only needs to process a subset of the transactions.
- State Channels: State channels allow you to move transactions off-chain, reducing the load on the main blockchain. This can improve scalability and reduce transaction fees.

Real-World Examples

- Ethereum 2.0: Ethereum is transitioning to a Proof-of-Stake (PoS) consensus mechanism and implementing sharding to improve its scalability.
- Lightning Network: The Lightning Network is a layer-2 scaling solution for Bitcoin that uses state channels to enable faster and cheaper transactions.
- Algorand: Algorand is a blockchain platform that uses a unique consensus mechanism and sharding to achieve high scalability and throughput.

By combining performance optimization techniques with appropriate scaling strategies, you can ensure that your Elixir blockchain can handle a growing number of users and transactions without sacrificing speed or efficiency.

9.4 Monitoring and Maintenance

Think of monitoring and maintenance as the mission control for your blockchain. You need to keep an eye on its vital signs, perform regular checkups, and address any issues that arise to prevent them from becoming major problems.

Monitoring: Keeping an Eye on the Vital Signs

Monitoring your blockchain involves collecting and analyzing data about its health and performance. This allows you to identify potential issues before they impact your users or the integrity of your blockchain.

Here are some key areas to monitor:

- System Metrics: Keep track of system-level metrics like CPU usage, memory usage, network traffic, and disk space. This helps you identify resource bottlenecks and ensure your nodes have enough capacity to handle the workload.
- Blockchain Metrics: Monitor blockchain-specific metrics like block height, transaction volume, transaction confirmation times, and network latency. This gives you insights into the health and performance of your blockchain network.
- Node Health: Monitor the health of individual nodes in your network. This might involve checking their connectivity, resource usage, and synchronization status.
- Security Events: Monitor for security-related events, such as suspicious activity, failed login attempts, and potential vulnerabilities.

Monitoring Tools

Fortunately, there are many tools available to help you monitor your blockchain:

- System Monitoring Tools: Use tools like Prometheus and Grafana to collect and visualize system metrics. These tools provide dashboards and alerts to help you identify and respond to issues quickly.
- Blockchain Explorers: Blockchain explorers provide a user-friendly interface for browsing and analyzing blockchain data. They can be used to monitor block height, transaction volume, and other key metrics.
- Logging: Collect and analyze logs from your blockchain nodes to identify errors, warnings, and other events that might indicate problems.

Maintenance: Keeping Your Blockchain in Top Shape

Maintenance involves performing regular tasks to ensure the smooth operation and longevity of your blockchain.

Here are some key maintenance tasks:

- Software Updates: Keep your blockchain software up-to-date with the latest security patches and bug fixes. This helps protect your network from vulnerabilities and ensures you're running the most stable and efficient version of the software.
- Hardware Upgrades: As your blockchain grows, you might need to upgrade your hardware to meet increasing demand. This might involve adding more memory, storage, or processing power to your nodes.

- Data Backup and Recovery: Regularly back up your blockchain data to prevent data loss in case of hardware failure, software issues, or security breaches.
- Security Audits: Conduct regular security audits to identify and address potential vulnerabilities in your blockchain's code and infrastructure.
- Performance Tuning: Periodically review and optimize your blockchain's performance. This might involve adjusting configuration parameters, optimizing your code, or upgrading your hardware.

Real-World Examples

- Infrastructure Monitoring: Cloud providers like AWS and Azure offer monitoring services that can be used to track the health and performance of your blockchain infrastructure.
- Blockchain Monitoring Services: Companies like Blockdaemon and Chainstack provide specialized monitoring services for blockchain networks.

Example: Monitoring Node Health with Elixir

```elixir
Elixir

defmodule NodeMonitor do

  use GenServer

  def start_link(node_address) do

    GenServer.start_link(__MODULE__, node_address, name: __MODULE__)

  end
```

```elixir
  def init(node_address) do
    # Schedule a recurring task to check the node's health
    schedule_work()
    {:ok, %{node_address: node_address}}
  end

  def handle_info(:check_health, state) do
    # Check if the node is reachable and responding
    case Node.ping(state.node_address) do
      :ok ->
        IO.puts("Node is healthy: #{state.node_address}")
      {:error, reason} ->
        IO.puts("Node is unhealthy: #{state.node_address}, reason: #{reason}")
        # Take corrective action, such as restarting the node or alerting an administrator
    end
    schedule_work()
    {:noreply, state}
  end

  defp schedule_work() do
```

```
    Process.send_after(self(), :check_health,
60_000) # Check every minute

  end

end
```

This example demonstrates a simple Elixir GenServer that periodically checks the health of a node.

By implementing a robust monitoring and maintenance strategy, you can ensure that your Elixir blockchain remains healthy, secure, and performant over the long term.

Chapter 10: The Future of Elixir and Blockchain

We've covered a lot of ground in this book, from the fundamentals of blockchain to building and deploying your own Elixir blockchain applications. But the blockchain world is constantly evolving, with new trends and innovations emerging all the time. In this final chapter, let's take a look at the exciting future of Elixir and blockchain and how they can continue to shape the decentralized landscape.

10.1 Emerging Trends in Blockchain

The blockchain space is a dynamic and ever-evolving landscape. New ideas and technologies are constantly emerging, pushing the boundaries of what's possible with this revolutionary technology. Let's explore some of the most exciting trends shaping the future of blockchain.

1. Layer-2 Scaling Solutions

One of the biggest challenges facing blockchain technology is scalability. As more users and applications adopt blockchain, the number of transactions can increase dramatically, leading to network congestion, slower transaction speeds, and higher fees.

Layer-2 scaling solutions aim to address this challenge by moving transactions off the main blockchain (Layer-1) to a secondary layer. This allows for faster and cheaper transactions while still maintaining the security and decentralization of the main blockchain.

Some popular Layer-2 solutions include:

- State Channels: We discussed state channels in Chapter 7. They allow participants to conduct multiple transactions off-chain and then settle the final result on the main blockchain.
- Rollups: Rollups bundle multiple transactions together and execute them off-chain. The results of these transactions are then submitted to the main blockchain as a single transaction, significantly reducing the on-chain load.

Examples:

- Lightning Network: A Layer-2 solution for Bitcoin that uses state channels to enable fast and cheap transactions.
- Optimistic Rollups: A type of rollup used on Ethereum that assumes transactions are valid unless challenged.
- ZK Rollups: Another type of rollup that uses zero-knowledge proofs to verify the validity of transactions off-chain.

2. Interoperability

The blockchain space is fragmented, with many different blockchains operating independently. Interoperability aims to bridge these different blockchains, allowing them to communicate and exchange value seamlessly.

This is like building bridges between different countries, enabling trade and collaboration.

Benefits of interoperability:

- Asset Transfer: Users can easily transfer assets and data between different blockchains.
- Collaboration: Different blockchain projects can work together and leverage each other's strengths.
- Unified Ecosystem: A more interconnected blockchain ecosystem fosters innovation and adoption.

Examples:

- Polkadot: A blockchain platform that connects different blockchains through a central "relay chain."
- Cosmos: Another platform that aims to create an "internet of blockchains" using a technology called IBC (Inter-Blockchain Communication).

3. Decentralized Finance (DeFi)

DeFi is revolutionizing the financial industry by creating decentralized alternatives to traditional financial services. This includes:

- Decentralized Exchanges (DEXs): Allow users to trade cryptocurrencies without intermediaries.
- Lending Platforms: Enable users to lend and borrow cryptocurrencies peer-to-peer.
- Stablecoins: Cryptocurrencies pegged to stable assets like the US dollar.
- Decentralized Insurance: Provides insurance services without traditional intermediaries.

Elixir's concurrency and fault-tolerance make it well-suited for building robust and scalable DeFi applications.

Examples:

- Uniswap: A popular decentralized exchange built on Ethereum.
- Aave: A decentralized lending platform.
- MakerDAO: A platform that issues DAI, a decentralized stablecoin.

4. Non-Fungible Tokens (NFTs)

NFTs are unique digital assets that represent ownership of digital or physical items. They're being used for:

- Art and Collectibles: Representing ownership of digital art, music, and other collectibles.
- Gaming: Creating unique in-game items and characters.
- Virtual Real Estate: Representing ownership of land in virtual worlds.
- Identity and Access Control: Representing digital identities and access rights.

Elixir can be used to build NFT marketplaces, minting platforms, and other NFT-related applications.

Examples:

- CryptoPunks: One of the first NFT projects, featuring unique pixel art characters.
- Bored Ape Yacht Club: A collection of 10,000 unique ape NFTs.

- Decentraland: A virtual world where users can buy and sell land represented as NFTs.

5. Metaverse and Web3

The metaverse is a persistent virtual world where users can interact with each other and digital assets. Web3 is a vision of a more decentralized internet powered by blockchain technology.

Elixir can play a role in building the infrastructure and applications for these emerging technologies, such as:

- Virtual World Platforms: Creating the backend systems for virtual worlds and metaverses.
- Decentralized Identity Systems: Building secure and decentralized identity management solutions.
- Web3 Infrastructure: Developing decentralized storage, communication, and computing platforms.

Examples:

- Sandbox: A virtual world where users can create and monetize gaming experiences.
- Decentraland: Another virtual world with a focus on user-owned content and experiences.

6. Privacy and Security

As blockchain adoption grows, privacy and security become even more critical. Emerging trends in this area include:

- Zero-Knowledge Proofs (ZKPs): Enabling private transactions and identity verification without revealing sensitive information.

- Confidential Transactions: Encrypting transaction details while maintaining blockchain integrity.
- Secure Multi-Party Computation (MPC): Allowing multiple parties to compute on data without revealing their individual inputs.

Elixir can be used to implement these techniques and build privacy-focused blockchain applications.

Examples:

- Zcash: A privacy-focused cryptocurrency that uses ZKPs.
- Secret Network: A blockchain platform that enables private smart contracts.

By staying informed about these emerging trends and leveraging Elixir's capabilities, you can be at the forefront of innovation in the blockchain space.

10.2 Elixir's Role in the Blockchain Ecosystem

Throughout this book, we've explored the powerful synergy between Elixir and blockchain technology. As we look towards the future, it's clear that Elixir is well-positioned to play a significant role in shaping the decentralized landscape. Let's examine why Elixir is such a compelling choice for blockchain development and how it can contribute to the growth and evolution of this exciting ecosystem.

Elixir's Strengths: A Perfect Match for Blockchain

Elixir possesses several inherent strengths that align perfectly with the demands of blockchain technology:

- Concurrency: Blockchain networks are inherently concurrent, with multiple nodes processing transactions and interacting with each other simultaneously. Elixir's concurrency model, based on lightweight processes and message passing, makes it exceptionally well-suited for handling these complex interactions efficiently and reliably.
- Fault-Tolerance: In a distributed system like a blockchain, failures are inevitable. Nodes can go offline, network connections can be disrupted, and unexpected errors can occur. Elixir's "let it crash" philosophy and OTP framework provide robust mechanisms for handling failures gracefully, ensuring that your blockchain applications remain stable and resilient.
- Scalability: As blockchain adoption grows, scalability becomes crucial. Elixir's ability to handle a large number of concurrent processes and its efficient resource management make it an excellent choice for building blockchain applications that can scale to meet increasing demand.
- Functional Programming: Elixir's functional programming paradigm promotes immutability, code clarity, and easier reasoning about program behavior. These characteristics are highly valuable in blockchain development, where security and correctness are paramount.

Elixir's Contributions to the Blockchain Ecosystem

Let's explore some specific ways Elixir can contribute to the blockchain ecosystem:

- Building Scalable and Reliable Infrastructure: Elixir can be used to build the core infrastructure for blockchain networks, including nodes, APIs, and backend services. Its concurrency and fault-tolerance ensure that these systems can handle high transaction volumes and remain stable even under stress.
- Developing High-Performance DApps: Elixir's efficiency and scalability allow you to create decentralized applications (DApps) that can handle a large number of users and complex interactions without sacrificing performance.
- Implementing Advanced Features: Elixir can be used to implement advanced blockchain features like state channels, cross-chain interoperability solutions, and privacy-enhancing techniques. Its flexibility and expressive power make it well-suited for tackling these complex challenges.
- Creating Developer-Friendly Tools: Elixir's clear syntax, powerful tooling, and active community contribute to a developer-friendly environment. This makes it easier to build, test, and maintain blockchain applications, fostering innovation and accelerating development.

Real-World Examples

While Elixir might not be as widely used in the blockchain space as some other languages, its adoption is growing, and there are already some notable examples of its use:

- Aeternity: A blockchain platform that uses Erlang (the language Elixir is built on) for its core infrastructure.
- Plasma: A Layer-2 scaling solution for Ethereum that has been implemented in Elixir.
- Ethereum: An Elixir library for interacting with the Ethereum blockchain.
- Libp2p: A modular peer-to-peer networking framework that has Elixir implementations and is used in various blockchain projects.

The Growing Elixir Community

The Elixir community is a vibrant and supportive group of developers who are passionate about the language and its potential. This community is actively contributing to the blockchain ecosystem by developing libraries, tools, and educational resources.

As the blockchain ecosystem continues to mature and evolve, Elixir is poised to play an even more significant role. Its strengths in concurrency, fault-tolerance, and scalability make it a natural fit for the demands of decentralized applications and infrastructure.

By continuing to learn and explore the possibilities of Elixir and blockchain, you can be at the forefront of this exciting technological frontier. Keep building, keep innovating, and keep pushing the boundaries of what's possible with these powerful technologies!

Conclusion

Congratulations! You've reached the end of your journey through the fascinating world of Elixir and blockchain. We've covered a lot of ground, from the fundamental concepts of blockchain technology to the intricacies of building and deploying decentralized applications with Elixir. You've learned about data structures like Merkle trees, cryptographic techniques like hashing and digital signatures, and consensus mechanisms that keep the blockchain secure and synchronized.

You've also seen how Elixir's unique features – concurrency, fault-tolerance, and functional programming – make it an ideal choice for tackling the challenges of blockchain development. You've built a basic blockchain from scratch, explored advanced features like state channels and cross-chain interoperability, and even dipped your toes into the world of decentralized applications (DApps).

By now, you should have a solid understanding of how Elixir and blockchain can work together to create innovative and impactful solutions. Whether you're interested in building decentralized applications, contributing to the development of blockchain infrastructure, or simply exploring the possibilities of this exciting technology, Elixir provides a powerful and versatile toolkit.

The blockchain space is constantly evolving, with new trends and innovations emerging all the time. Stay curious, keep learning, and continue to explore the vast potential of Elixir and blockchain. Engage with the vibrant Elixir and blockchain communities, contribute to open-source projects, and share your knowledge with others.

Building a Decentralized Future

Blockchain technology has the potential to revolutionize many aspects of our lives, from finance and healthcare to supply chain management and governance. By combining the power of Elixir with the transformative potential of blockchain, you can be a part of building a more decentralized, transparent, and equitable future.

So, go forth and build amazing things! The world is waiting for your innovative ideas and your Elixir-powered blockchain solutions.

www.ingramcontent.com/pod-product-compliance
Lightning Source LLC
Chambersburg PA
CBHW082248220526
45469CB00009B/2915